Our Ever Changing World:
Through the Eyes of Artists:

Best of 2016
Art & Story
California

2016

Coordinated by Karrie Ross

Our Ever Changing World ~ Best of 2016 Art & Story Book 6
Coordinated by Karrie Ross

A Be-It-Now! Book

Printed in the United States of America
Books are available for special promotions and premiums.
For details contact:
Published by Be It Now!®, Los Angeles, CA 90247
email: books@beitnow.com
book website: www.karrieross.com
http://www.oureverchangingworld.com

Book Design: www.KarrieRoss.com
ALL imagery is © per respective artist. All rights reserved by artist.

ISBN 13:9781546652458

To my native state, California.

To all the Artists, who participated.

For all the wonders of the world.

Thank you

Other Books by Karrie Ross

The Big Little Book of Thoughs
My Breasts Talking
My Hands Talking
My Trees Talking

Coaching Parent Coaching Child:
3x award winning book on Parenting

Got Shui? Tips and Transformations
Got Shui? Energy Phases

The Bebuddies.com Books

Be Watchful: EnviroNate (*award winning book*)
Be Healthy: Doc
Be Kind: CareyAngel

Books by BzzzBee.com the Bee
BZZZed
You Have My Heart
SnowBee

Our Ever Changing World:
Through the Eyes of Artists:

Book One: What are you Saving from Extinction?
Book Two: Couples and Collaborations
Book Four: Artists, ART, & Story
Book Five: Idle Chatter: What's in your Cupboard...
Book Six: Best of 2016 Art & Story, California
Book Seven: Best of 2017 Art & Story, USA
Book Eight: Signs of the Times, Ann Marie Rouseau

INTRODUCTION

*~ an introduction deals with the subject of the book,
supplementing and introducing the text and indicating a point of
view to be adopted by the reader. ~*

I BELIEVE THAT ARTISTS ARE IN SOME WAY HISTORIANS...that their work saves something from becoming forgotten...and changes lives and perspectives.

This book series documents by the year—I tried other ways but yearly seems to work out best. The saying "Art examples Life" is very true and can been seen yearly and sometimes major change within a story that happened in that year to affect the artists creative state of being.

Again to those new to my books, I am a native to California so many of them are only of California artists. There will be some books that extend to other locations over time.

Please enjoy the read.

> Thank you.
> Karrie Ross
> http://www.karrieross.com
> http://www.oureverchangingworld.com

Note: I appologize if I left anyone out anywhere or misscoppied anything. The book has not been edited or proofed, so sentence structure is purely of the artists own words and adds to the quality of the sharing. THANK each and every one of the artists that I asked to change a word here-or-there OR to rewrite the whole story. Your efforts have not gone unappreciated and help to make this book the best it can be.

Artists

Listing of Artists in Order of Appearence

Cindy Betzer Pharis 11

Cindy Rinne 14

Debbi Swanson Patrick . .17

Diane-Cockerill 20

Douglas Eisenstark 23

Ellen Riingen 26

Jeff Hilbers 29

Jim Salvati 31

Karen Kauffman 33

Karin Skiba 36

Barbara Kerwin 38

Laurel Paley 42

Linda Sue Price 46

Lorraine Bubar 48

Mara Thompson 50

Mara Zaslove 53

Martin Cox 56

Melissa Ann Lambert 59

Michelle D. Ferrera 62

Milo Reice 64

Peter Hess 67

Ron Therrio 70

Scott A. Trimble 73

Sharon Suhovy 77

Simone Gad 79

Skye Amber Sweet 81

Susan Lizotte 84

Suzanne Budd 86

Tomoaki Shitbata 89

Tracey Weiss 91

Randi Matushevitz 94

Karrie Ross 96

Best of 2016

Art & Story

California

Cindy Betzer Pharis

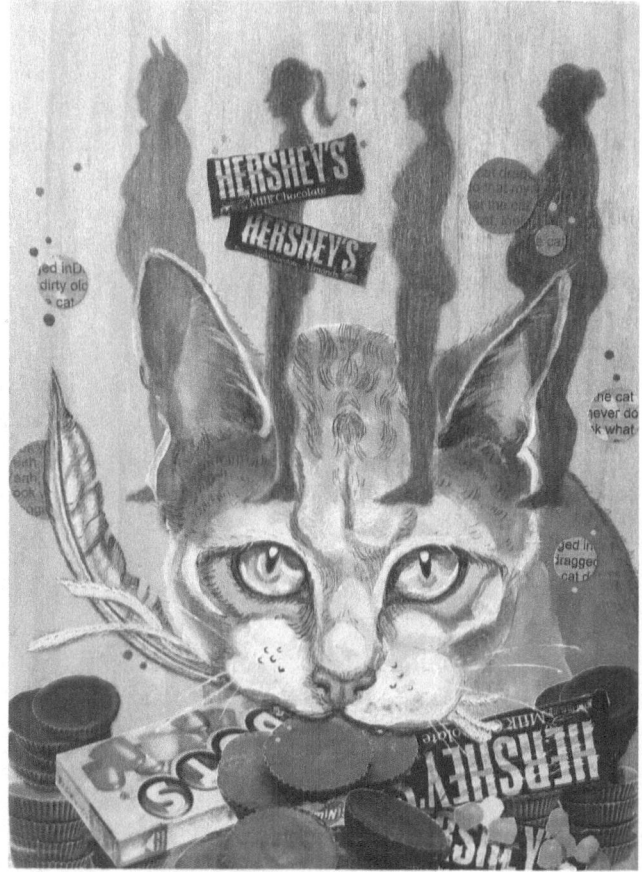

Look What The Cat Dragged in - 2

LOOK WHAT THE CAT DRAGGED IN-2

2016 was the year I turned sixty. My body began to emphasize the changes: cautionary diagnoses by doctors, not standing straight, and weight change. I tackled this through exercise, achieving various goals, tossing out unnecessary stress, and eating well. The more I tried to eat well, the stronger my cravings became for chocolate, cheese, and tortilla chips with salsa. So there was this constant yo-yoing that summarized most of the year. I started listening to excuses I was making: "but, it was on sale," "I work hard, I deserve this, all of it," "Eating healthily is boring, why start following the rules now," and the main one, "It was there," or "Gee, look what the cat dragged in."

The cat is bringing in temptation, and it is one to avoid. So I started playing with the words, the friendly, helpful cat, the thin/heavy body image, and the greatest temptation for me: chocolate. As I worked on the projects, the realization solidified: I have been fighting temptation not only in the year 2016, but my entire life. I befriend the cat that brings the gifts. The cat isn't a stranger at a random door. I've fed, encouraged, petted, and dropped bits of chicken leading to my entrance. Why are my desires not what is best for me? "I am my own worst enemy." Why can I intellectualize what is in my best interest, but I have young behaviors that are more powerful and at the same time, self-destructive? How do I heal this rift, and cross the bridge into self-realization?

2016 is a healing year, I can contemplate the many birds and gifts dragged to my front door, and I don't wonder how the cat found my door. I painted my address on its paws. It's as if my past is in slow motion, I begin to see the weaving, and how I sheared the lambs and carded the wool. The temptress didn't randomly find my weakness, I made a little cat saddle and bridle, and rode through the night.

The edge of temptation, the tip of the wave, the exhilaration of no moment being more important, the sigh of relief when it is passed, and the despair when I dove deeply only to discover the ship had sailed. Temptation, passion, weakness, strength, and discipline are a continuous rotation.

The painting is autobiographical, and symbolizes a day in the life of a sixty year-old woman in 2016. It is acrylic, ink, and collage on wood. The woman in the background changes from the cat to the woman and from heavy to thin. In this sense, the woman maintains her power, not only is she tempted, but she is the temptress. The cat holds a lovely assortment of tempting chocolate, Dots, and has recently eaten a bird. The circles are filled with the Rolling Stones' lyrics:

Oh my god look what the cat dragged in
Livin' my life sin after sin
Night rolls up and I do it again
Oh my god, look what the cat dragged in
And look what the cat dragged in
Don't you call me a friend
Get out of my house with your dirty old mouth
Take yourself out again

Oh my god look what the cat dragged in
Livin' my life sin after sin
Night rolls up and I do it again
Oh my god, look what the cat dragged in
And look what the cat dragged in
Don't you call me a friend
Get out of my house with your dirty old mouth
Take yourself out again

http://www.portraitsandart.com

Cindy Rinne

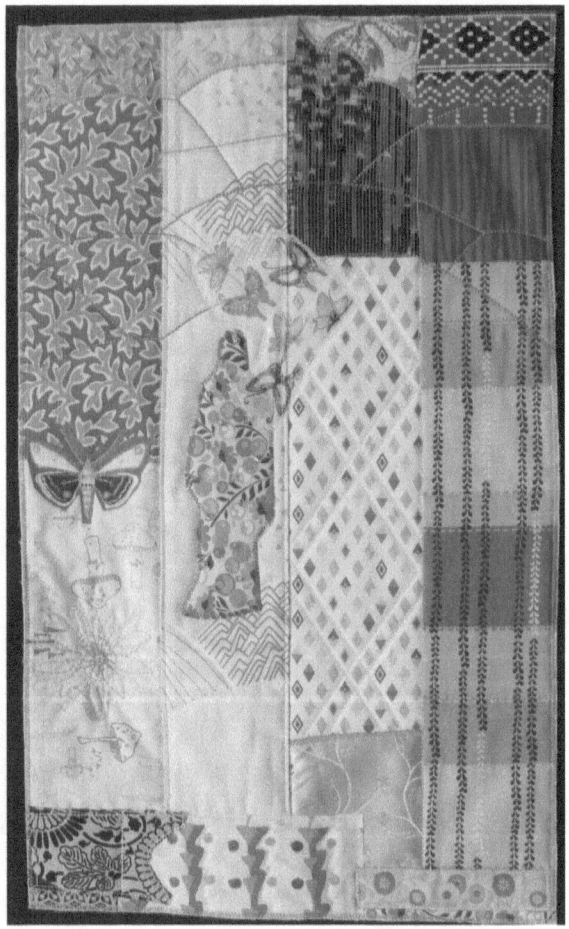

In The Garden of my Heart

In The Garden Of My Heart - January 2016

A friend told me she had taken a Kundalini Yoga class. I didn't know what it was. I practiced Hatha Yoga. I decided to trust her and give this new form a try. One class and I fell in love. The teacher had a deep passion for this practice to move prana, chant, and a gong bath. It was hard to repeat or hold poses in asanas for different purposes—like opening your heart. Chanting Sanskrit and the gong vibrated my bones long after the class.

Every Tuesday night I drove the 215 to the 91 freeway to yoga class. A 25-30 minute drive usually with traffic to get to class. Same roads, same time, same day of the week, every week. After the 60 interchange, the freeway always opened up for a time. I would go from the fast lane to the slow lane with ease.

One winter evening there seemed to be several accidents enroute and ahead of me. As I passed the interchange, I began to do my usual lane changes and picking up speed. I suddenly realized that traffic was stopped. I slammed my breaks in the slow lane. The car in front of me was safe, but my older car didn't stop and began to skid. I tried to steer to the side and stop. Instead, my car began to spin out of control across the 91 freeway. My windshield was dry, but the road unseen in the dark was wet and slick.

Once I realized there was nothing more I could do, I closed my eyes and sent up a quick prayer. All I saw was medium gray. No shining light. No darkness. Just the calm of gray. Then a car hit me. Not hard, but I crashed into the medium.

In Kundalini Yoga we begin each class with a chant for protection. Sometimes this is said before driving a car. I grew up Catholic believing in Guardian Angels. I cannot explain, but I do believe something or someone (totems?) watched over me. My car was undriveable. I got out in the drumming carpool lane without a scratch or a torn muscle. I figured I was meant to live to attend my daughter's upcoming wedding and my son's visit. To make it to my 42nd Anniversary.

The passenger in the other car was screaming, "What were you doing?" Over and over again. As calmly as I could, I explained I lost control and did not try to hit her or this wall. She seemed unhurt, just angry. The driver was not ok, then ok, and later had whiplash. Help came in the form of the Freeway Service Patrol, husbands, and firemen.

A new, safer car. I forced myself to drive that same road again to yoga class. Creating new fiber art after this incident, here I am sparkling with gratitude. I am walking in the foothills enjoying the vistas of sky, trees, and vines. Butterflies swirl and speak. A moth guards. Mushrooms reveal hidden places and flowers bloom. I take deep breaths and chant to the sky. I combine fabrics from Japan, France, Nigeria, and Indonesia. Also, from several friends as my heart continues to expand.

www.fiberverse.com

Debbi Swanson Patrick

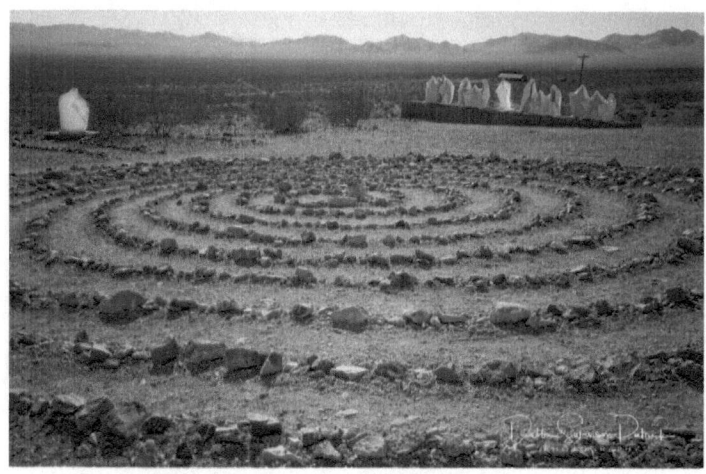

In 2016 I began to recover. Back and leg pain plagued me since college and in 2012 it all came to a head. A series of spinal surgeries, hip replacement, knee surgery began in 2013, the last being lower spinal fusion January 2016.

Having so many physical issues makes me long for "ahh-hhhh" of the outdoors. A change of scenery is really good when you're in pain. I'm no extreme hiker or anything like that, but I am a yogi and love trips to get out in nature. In 2016 the destination was Death Valley—twice—for two "super" experiences.

First, we went for the Super Bloom in the spring. Who says there's no weather in Death Valley! We experienced sun, clouds, wind, rain, sleet, and hail in just two days. Got the sun and hail at the same time as we descended into the valley from a trip to Beatty and Rhyolite. A vast carpet of yellow and purple flowers welcomed us as we drove, stopping periodically to shoot. The wind made it difficult to get perfectly still flowers but I tried.

Badwater, the lowest point in the U.S. at 282 feet below sea level, and usually a dry salty plain, was dotted with small turquoise ponds. Not enough to kayak in as in some years, but enough to feel completely different than usual. I walked out a ways on the flat plain but couldn't manage the weight of my camera gear, so I didn't go far. The walk up to the viewing area for Zabriske Point required a cane and boyfriend's arm. Still, it felt good to do it.

We enjoyed a lot of time at the Furnace Creek Ranch golf course bar, watching The Hulk, Superman, a ballerina, and other characters play a round. The Hulk even rode up to the bar and drove off with his beer in hand. Turned out to be a cos-tume-required family reunion! Now that's a family I'd like to be part of. I also swam as much as I could in the warm spring-fed pool. If there's a heaven on earth, that pool is it for me! Another couple was in the pool that night—a fellow artist and her hus-band. We had instant connection over talk of spirit and the Aramaic language. She could see the spirit of my late husband with me as we shivered in the cold wind. We exchanged cards and are still in touch.

In November we went back with a photo group led by pal Keith Skelton for the Super Moon rise. I could get around a lit-tle better this time. Our group of photographers waited atop the breathtaking Ubehebe Crater for the moon to peek out from behind distant mountains. Frankly, I was a little disap-pointed. I expected it to be huge. To me it was just a little larg-er than normal. Beautiful, but not the WOW I wanted. Instead of great moon shots I got abstract landscapes of patterns, shapes, and colors that I love.

On this trip to Badwater, I experienced another first. At dawn, a small plane flew overhead and low, right over us and on up the valley. It was probably a ranger, and fun to see in those usually vacant skies. The entire line of us photographers all had our cameras trained on that plane until it disappeared.

My favorite images from both trips were taken in Rhyolite, more specifically the Goldwell Open Air Museum, an outdoor sculpture park located just before you enter the Nevada ghost town. Created by a group of prominent Belgian artists, led by the late Albert Szukalski, new artists now work there through the nearby Red Barn Art Center.

The images make you wonder where the hell you are. You can see a giant man with a hammer from the main road, and perhaps the giant pink lady called Lady Desert: The Venus of Nevada by Dr. Hugo Heyrman.

The main sculpture that started it all is that of The Last Supper in ghost form. The figure on the left is the "artist," and it changes periodically as the sculptor repairs or updates what the artist is carrying in his hand. This time it was a new palette of paint. In the spring he carried upright tubes of paint in red, yellow, white and blue. This shot includes the meditative labrynth with the artist facing his creation, the figures of The Last Supper, with Jesus in the center, and the telephone pole cross in the background of the Mojave Desert.

I never really saw the totality of this view until I took this photo, now presumably seeing the sculptor's vision. And the weather makes it more exciting. You want to be up here when dark moody clouds threaten rain but pinholes allow the sun to shine through. It's a religious experience!

Now the old crumbling buildings are sculptures, too, joining the oversized mosaic couch, the bottle house with its mini version of the old town, and The Last Supper.

For me, healing continues, pain must be managed and while that's a 24/7 effort, I'm grateful for outings like these that are full of visual surprises.

www.debbiswansonpatrick.com

Diane Cockerill

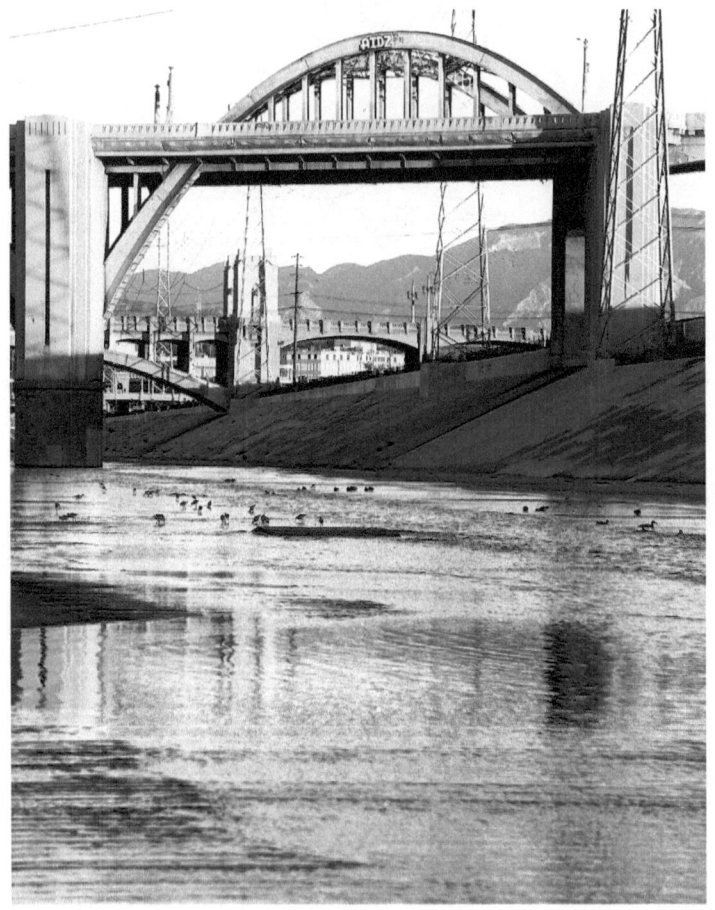

New Year's Morning, 2016

A chance to experience solitude in Los Angeles is a rarity. Major holidays afford an opportunity to move about freely with minimal human contact and light traffic, so my husband and I took advantage of the New Year's morning and drove toward downtown Los Angeles with the idea of reaching the Los

Angeles River in time for the first sunrise of 2016. The Arts District gave the impression of an abandoned ghost town on that quiet morning as we headed up Santa Fe Avenue to the opening of the eerie tunnel under the historic Sixth Street Bridge, still standing in all its glory.

The tunnel's opening beckoned us, and although we originally planned to walk through the tunnel to the river, the challenge of driving down the narrow concrete enclosure was too tempting. Fortunately there were no cars or people surprising us at the top of the ramp. I had traveled down the tunnel countless times but always in daylight. On a typical day, the river scene would have been crowded with other photographers, homeless characters, cars doing doughnuts, and photo shoots.

New Year's Day presented a completely different experience. I caught my breath as the tranquil scene presented itself before my eyes. The pre-dawn view was enchanting as the darkness hid any signs of civilization except for the lights on the many bridges that cross the river; their outlines barely perceptible. It was uncharacteristically cold, even for a January morning, and leaving the warmth of the heated car was difficult but the chance to photograph this spectacular scene propelled me to grab my cameras and seize the moment.

Not a soul in sight as we drove up and down the river's edge. Sweet silence enveloped us. We had the Los Angeles River all to ourselves except for the water fowl, oblivious to the world around them as they poked in the flowing waters searching for early morning treats. Sunrise slowly showed her hand and I quickly photographed the deep purples and blues giving way to warmer colors appearing and intensifying as seconds passed. The bridges, banks, water and skies were soon painted with soft pink and orange then burst into brilliant gold and vermilion with the rise of the morning sun, illuminating the rippling water flow. Colorful graffiti appeared as sunlit drawings on the banks. I was a subject in a magnificent watercolor painting, pigments created by Mother Nature.

I took the time to look around, absorb the magnificence of the dawning of a brand new year and felt gratitude for the special connection to the river, alive and vibrant, flowing just for us that one glorious morning.

https://www.facebook.com/dianecockerill

Douglas Eisenstark

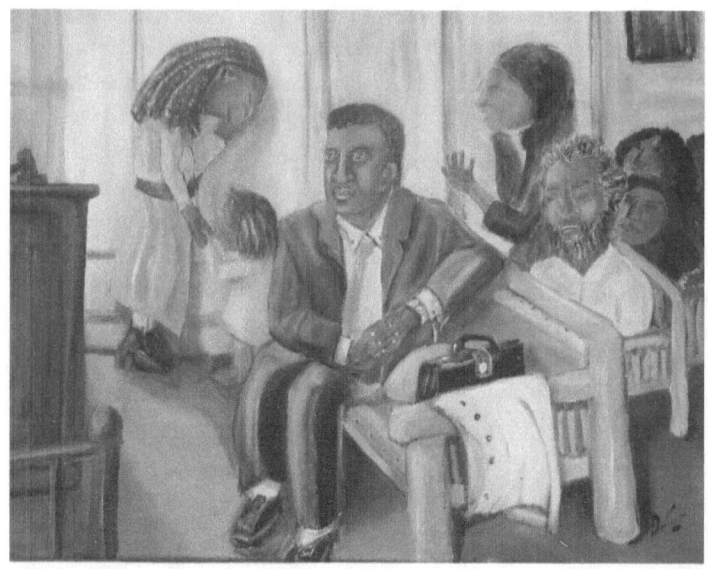

The Faux Sho's have been quite a challenge. I am sure I am not alone in not quite understanding what we are doing. At times the theme requires a counter argument, other times it will push our technical abilities to

make faithful reproductions. Romanticism was a struggle while when we moved into Expressionism then my skill (and lack of it) could approach the work on its own terms. 20th Century art movements often had solid themes that we could approach with our own concerns and contemporary issues. Perhaps the economics, the intent and freedoms of art making had become contemporary and more closely matched our own. As David Scott points outs in his book, "Art: Authenticity, Restoration, Forgery" that what is fake and what is authentic is a cultural, financial and political web. Is a religious painting in a museum complete if priests, nuns and devotees not allowed to light candles and kneel in front of it? The Faux Sho's allows the artist a freedom in the restraint of the limitation. The theme frees the desire and necessity for "originality" and creative interpretation becomes the source of the artistic impulse.

For the "Social Realism" Faux Sho' Show I chose the Soviet courtroom painting Drama in Soviet Court (1955) by A. Solodovnikov. What I tried to capture most about the painting was the lawyers eyes and the hidden/half/almost sneer of his lips. In those features of the face we feel the disgust and the injustice. The young mother (the convicted's wife?) and his child weep in the background. Injustice, despair and outrage are all there without showing a policeman, a judge or even the defendant. I had to re-work the lawyer's face many, many times. The original has him twisting his body and head in a way that eluded me. I can only hope some day to paint in the "social realism" style. The social I can get, the realism eludes my technical ability. (My MFA is in film not painting!)

This was the third in a series of paintings I have been making about incarcerated persons. Like most people being put in jail is undoubtedly my greatest fear. Being innocent of a crime and incarcerated seems an unimaginable nightmare. (For that reason I often give what I can to the Innocence Project which works to free people who have been unfairly put in jail.)

While painting this I was trying to invoke a story I heard about a young man in Watts, Los Angeles who had unwittingly broken his parole and was re-sentenced to years in jail. Pleas from friends, his wife and his young children fell on the deaf and cruel ears of the prosecutor. So in this case I used updated Social Realism to reflect our own times. The Solodovnikov painting is post-Stalin of a Stalin era trial, meaning of course he could probably show it in his time hopefully without repercussions. "Making modern" the painting doesn't require a knowledge of Stalin era injustice and so the painting can stand alone with reference to an admittedly rather obscure older painting. In this case, the older is simply reference without interpretation.

There is often an uneasiness to copying others in these Faux Sho's. They are fun but do we copy or do we interpret? Are we honoring or are we parodying? For a time I tried to do only woman artists, For the Dada Show I picked the African American, David Hammons. I approached the Dada with the modern "dada-istic" artist David Hammons basketball works. Is this an unfair "appropriation" of an African American's work with its decidedly social and political content. (And this was pre-Whitney 2017 show.) What is tribute to black struggle and what is "stealing" And then stepping back, this is after all: a "Faux Show" for Pete's sake. My trade-off was to add a living plant. Maybe my conscious wouldn't allow me to be as pessimistic as the chains suggested. In any case I look forward to the next one!

www.taiqi.me

Ellen Riingen

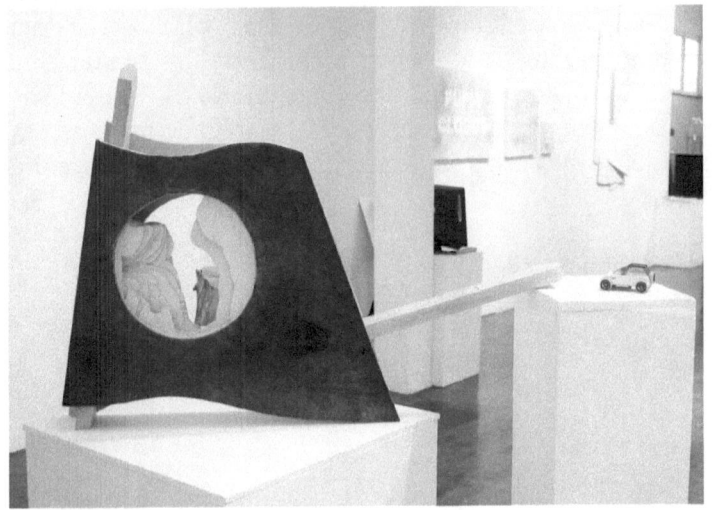

The Hole In The Wall

The year of 2016 will go down as the year of drastic changes, not just for our country but for me personally. This was the year I decided to give up my nearly 20-year career in architecture to do something completely different. The decision resonated with me down to my core. I knew I was ready. Just about the time I made the internal commitment to let go of my career investment, I received an email from a good friend to be in an art show that he was curating. It was divine timing. I was thrilled. I didn't have many answers on where I would be going next in life, but what I did know was that I wanted to do this show. And that is all I needed to know.

The show was called "If I Were A Carpenter" curated by Steve Fujimoto where he wanted to blur the lines between art, craft, and utility. I was thrilled to throw myself in the art of making and meaning, a concept early on in my architectural schooling. As I mulled through ideas for my art piece, I remembered that this wasn't the first time in my life that I made a drastic career change. I've done it once before when I changed from advertising to architecture through a series of seemingly synchronized life events.

There has always been a part of me not of this world who always seems to remind me that we are not our jobs; we are a collection of experiences leading us towards a higher conscious of knowing. It was time for me to test that sense with faith.

About the time of my first career change, I hit the road towards the majestic American Southwest deserts to connect back with nature....and that part of me not of this world, my spirit. The desert has always been that place for me to be alone with God and Nature. I visited four states making my rounds from the Painted Desert, the Petrified Forest, Monument Valley, Chaco Canyon. They were all great memories for me, but one place in particular both surprised and moved me. My spirit and the spirit of this place resonated to the same frequencies. I felt a oneness here.

This place was the lesser known Canyon de Chelly National Monument located on the high plateau in northeastern Arizona near the center of the Navajo Reservation of the Four Corners. From an aerial view, the canyon looks like a giant gorge cut in the earth where the sandstone walls are a near-vertical plunge. Not until one gets closer to look below can one see rivers of green foliage and streams below cutting through these striated red walls. The walls were shaped by the multi-directional winds to beautifully sculpted coves. Unlike other national monuments, I saw signs of everyday life such as livestock, small earthen homes, agricultural crops, and Navajo ranchers on horseback. I found out later that only a handful of Navajo families still live there. Their energy and its history felt strong here. No one was allowed down in the canyon without being accompanied by a park ranger or a designated Navajo guide, so off I went to find my guide. Well preserved are the historical markings still left in and on the sandstone from the tribes that were there before the Navajo Indians. The ruins of the ancient Anasazi Indian cliff dwellings still remain tucked away within the massive walls. The daily connection with nature remained strong here, both then and now. It was a beautiful visit with simple yet profound inhabitants. I ended up spending a few days there attempting to soak up as much of that energy that I could possibly bring back to Southern California.

At this new junction in my life for my second career change in 2016, I went back in my mind to those days and the energy I felt there. As I said good-bye to my architecture life, I wanted to take with me the great and delicate responsibility I learned of being co-creators with Nature as we build things or live our everyday lives. I wanted my art piece to remind us that the simplest common building materials such as the 2x4 stud or plywood sheathing we so easily pull from the store came from another living thing. Its humble presence has energy and a story. We just need to be stop, be quiet, and listen.

http://ellenriingen.com

Jeff Hilbers

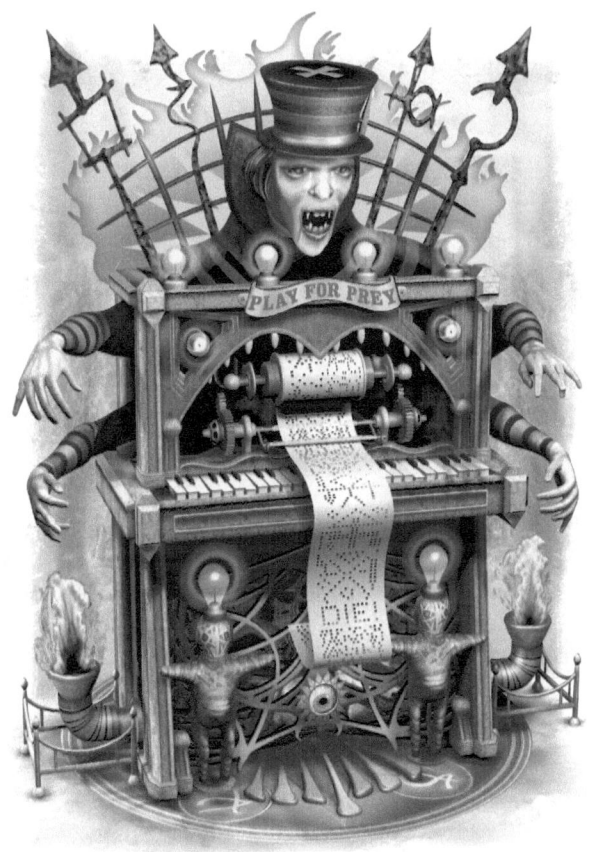

Siren Song

The Siren Song

The Demonic Piano (or Satan's Pianoforte) is a highly prized item for collectors of disturbing, dangerous, and possibly evil musical instuments.

The were produced from 1885 to 1890 by a somewhat deranged member of the Steinway family. He had been disowned by the family, and in his childhood was referred to as "Wrongway Steinway".

Wrongway Steinway set up shop in Paris, and embarked on a career of rather unusual instrument construction. He is credited with the invention of the anal harmonica, and a guitar that could be played by a dog.

Wrongway became fascinated by player pianos, and produced perhaps 500 of these fine instruments. They became infamous in Continental society, and many were sold to insane asylums. They were also highly prized in the courts of hereditarily crazy European monarchs. Historians often refer to the Demonic Piano as being "a culturally destabilizing influence," and say that it helped incite World War One.

The company's motto was "Comfort the Afflicted, and Afflict the Comfortable." This fine sentiment was actually realized, in that the insane enjoyed it, and nobody else did, until they went insane.

Many of these pianos were destroyed during and after the First War. Some were burned by angry mobs (torches and pitchforks). In other cases, the owner of the piano lit himself on fire and ran at the thing.

Perhaps thirty of these pianos are still in existence. Documentation is difficult since nobody wants to admit that they have one. There is speculation that most are, or have been, owned by authoritarian dictators around the world.

Research indicates that Papa Doc Duvalier, Idi Amin, Joseph Stalin, Imelda Marcos, Pol Pot, Pinochet, and J. Edgar Hoover have been proud owners over the years.

New owners should be mindful that maintenance is an issue with an instrument like this. It's power is derived from a very specific chemical compound, which involves mixing brimstone with holy water and jello pudding (wear a raincoat).

Anyone hearing the music from this instrument should be diapered and in a straight jacket, or under heavy sedation.

http://jeffhilbers.com/

Jim Salvati

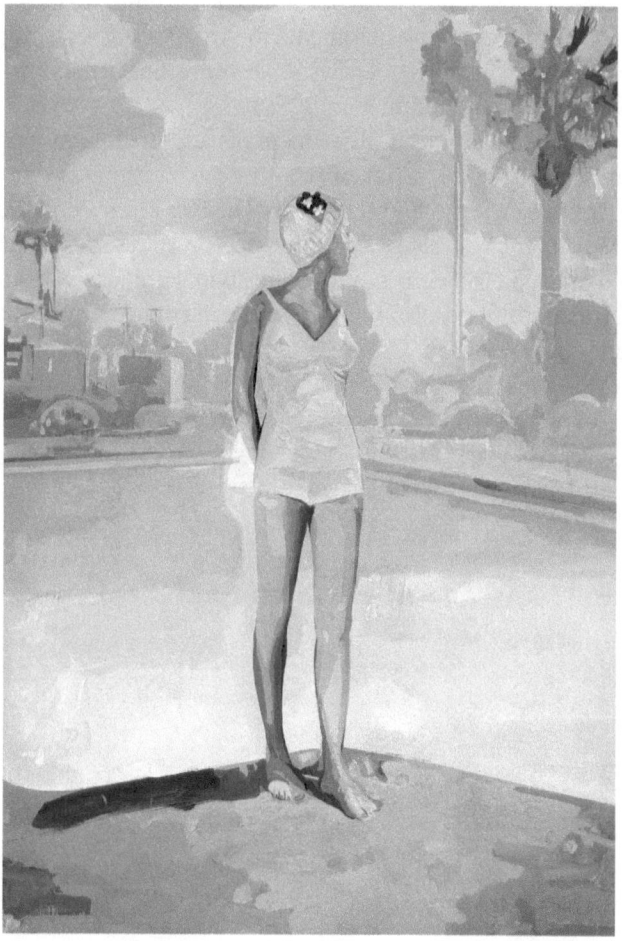

Bathing Cap

Sitting next to my southern California pool, water, whether a swimming pool or the ocean is my playground. As a kid, I was aptly nick-named Fish. Swimming pools have always been part of my life and almost an every day event in my youth.

I received a call last year from a long time friend that curates and once managed the Bellagio Masters Fine Art

Gallery in Las Vegas. Monet's, Renoir's and Van Gogh's filled the gallery. I was asked to show my work in the Monet Room. That was almost ten years ago. Carolyn called me in 2016 to be part of her group showing at Miami Art Basel. I was in great company with Jean-Michel Basquiat and other artists in their group that I greatly admire.

My love of Vintage California pools and great family photo albums influenced a series of paintings, which this is one in a series of five called, "Bathing Cap." The San Francisco Modern Art Movement was also a big influence on this series of paintings based off of colors and a lifestyle familiar to me. An Additional influence for me in 2016 was a trip up north to document artist Nathan Oliveria's work at Stanford University. That was a real turning point in my work and the direction that I will explore for future pieces.

: http://www.salvatidesign.com

Karen Kauffman

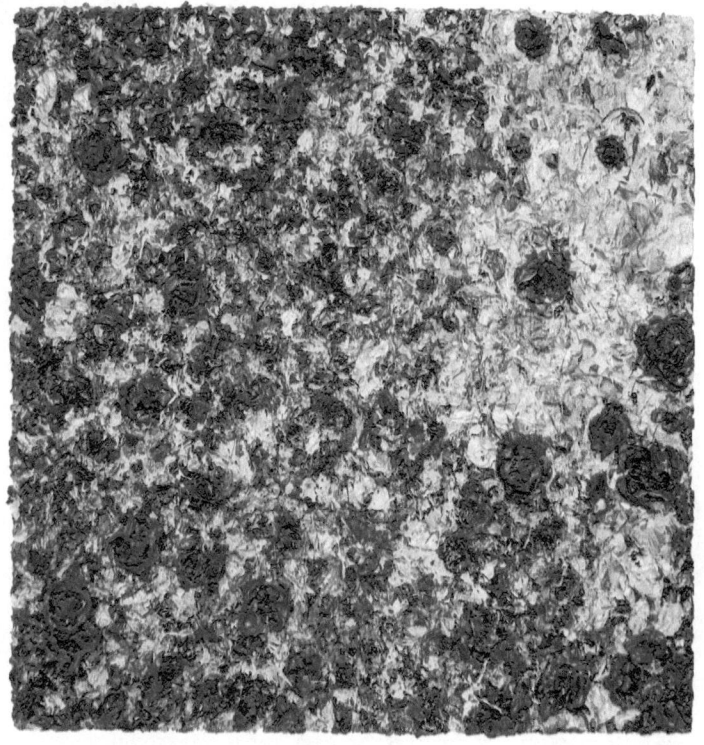

I had known my mother-in-law since I was 10 years old, and now were waiting for her to come home from the hospital, again, but this time we were there to meet with Hospice. This was on the day of my 60th birthday. Two days later, she was gone from this world. This past year, especially, we had completely reversed roles of parent and child. My husband and I had become caretakers of an aging parent, one who wanted to "live to 101 years, just like (her) daddy". We had raised 3 sons, but I had no idea that this era of life would be much more taxing. Over the past 10 years, we had cared for her, but this was definitely the roughest year. Over the course of 2016, I started painting this piece little by little, making marks, much like finger painting but in 3-D, letting each curved shape of gel medium dry and build upon itself, layer by layer. I had to work in small blocks of time, because it seemed that I had so little time to myself, especially studio time. I just did whatever I could in small bursts of creativity. I had originally set out to paint a larger version of a similar one that I had done to commemorate a dear friend whom I had lost earlier. I hadn't suspected that we would also be saying good-bye to my mom-in-law this same year and this painting would mark another loss of a loved one. I had thought that my husband's retirement 5 years earlier, from a 30-year career as a firefighter/fire captain in East Los Angeles would be one of complete relaxation and continuous travel, throw all of our cares to the wind. That did not happen. Things may not always go the way you've planned, but the good news/bad news is that you can always count on change itself. I would not have changed our circumstances, for the most part anyway. She and I were extremely close and I know that she would have done the same for me. She left us with so much to remember. I had mentioned that I had known her since I was 10, that's because she had been my favorite 5th grade Sunday School teacher. She was an independent and outspoken woman, a bit of a rebel, and under no uncertain terms, she did not like pretentious people. I loved that "Mom" would speak her mind, even if it wasn't especially well received. Although sometimes what she said was cringe-worthy, we often found the humor in it. She was fascinated by desert flowers in the springtime, so we would make trips out to our southern California desert in Joshua Tree, so she could see them up close and personal. Her special name for the many varieties was generally, "Belly Flowers", because, according to her, "you had to get down on your belly to see them", since most were so tiny. This always reminded me of my favored Georgia O'Keeffe quote, "Nobody sees a flower-really-it is so small it takes time-we haven't the time-and to see takes time, like to have a friend takes time." So in circular fashion, my mind wandered back again to my dear friend, then to all of the women in my life who have meant so much to me, in a chain-reaction of thoughts. With every brushstroke, drip, or flick of paint, I often think about my friendships, every relationship whether close or far reaching, and what's happening in our world. The slideshow is of our struggles, pain, triumphs, strength, our common ground, shared laughter. My thoughts continue full range through birth and death and all of what life entails in this grand epic story. And with each mark on the canvas that I make, it becomes a metaphor for each choice in life that I make, every adaptation to change, every small meaningful action that contributes to the whole, building a life. Nothing stays the same, for better or for worse. So I watch, I try to look closely, openly, much like looking at the Belly Flowers.

www.karenkauffman.com

Karin Skiba

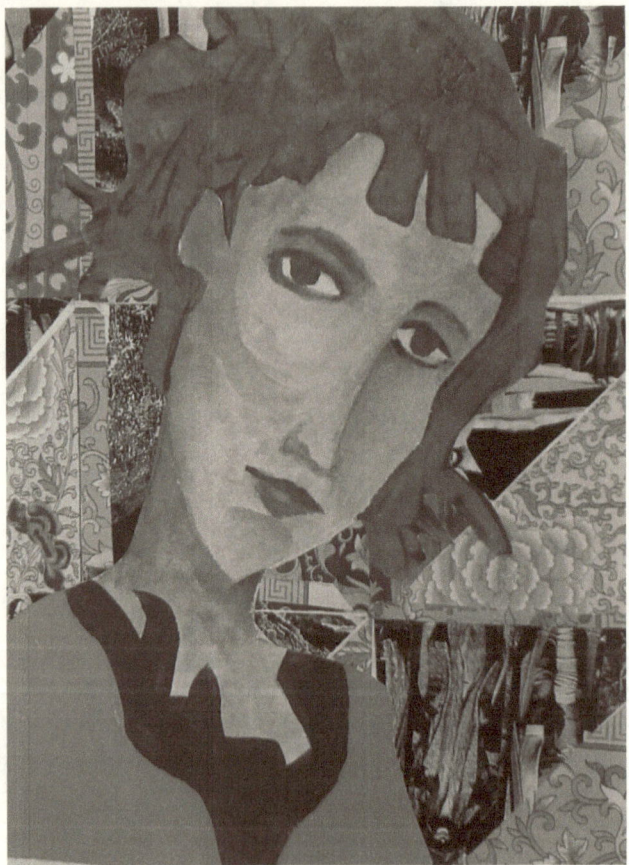

Reluctant Verona, detail

Last year was an amazing, enlightening time for this artist. My mother died in January and left me to pack up her life, distribute her worldly goods, as well as bury her in mother earth. I became the matriarch in my family to replace her. Mortality became a realization more than ever before, and of course this had its reverberations.

I went to my studio in Joshua Tree every week following the ceremonies and family stuff, and began to paint small portraits of women. That is my "go to" when I am doing art for myself with no intellectual restrictions. It is totally reflexive.

Drawing from photos in books or magazines, working very freely with a blue oil pastel on panel, I then brought out the oil paint and immersed myself in this new group of invented personalities.

Blue has been a color I turn to, for some reason, in a lot of my art work, and these portraits, begun with blue drawing material, all featured blue faces. It seemed totally reasonable to me and felt comfortable.

In July, I had a small exhibit in the desert at a little gallery with these works. I called it VAGRANT ANGELS. People reacted strongly to the blue skinned women! Why are they blue, are you sad? I could not say I was particularly sad or that this work was a reflection of my mom, and I knew I was dealing with my grief, being alone in the studio for days on end. However, I was kind of surprised at this reaction. And realized it was an obvious interpretation, embarrassing in a way. Vulnerability revealed.

The blue ladies are now a reminder of last year and how I worked through my loss, in the company of ANGELS.

https://www.facebook.com/karin.m.skiba?ref=br_rs

Barbara Kerwin

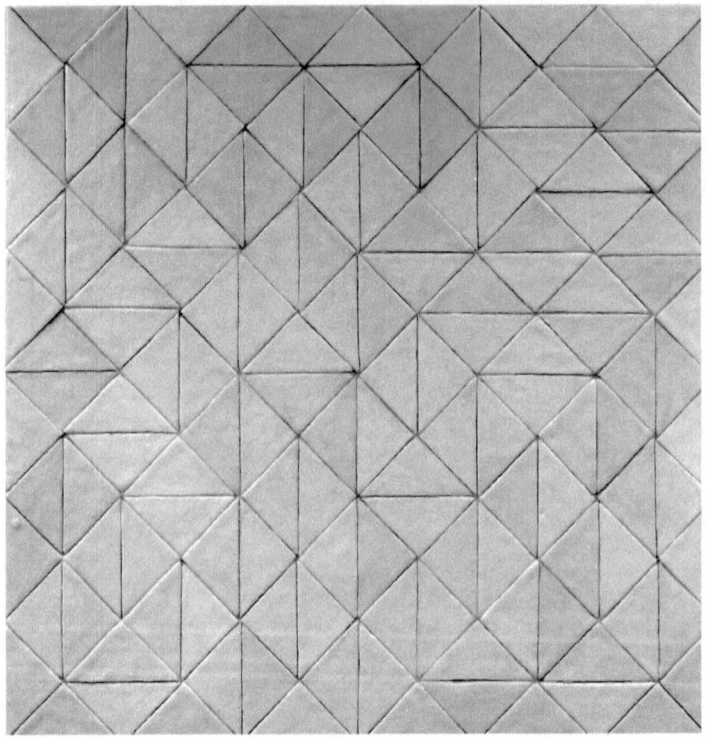

I Know Where I'm Going

On Going

The Olympics created a rain that moved down the mountain everyday at naptime on our 160-acre wilderness ranch. I'd sneak from my bed and press my nose and hands against the old, rolled-glass windows and watch the show!

The contrast between mountain living without electricity, with only wood stoves and kerosene lamps, outhouses and animals—to moving into the city, could not have been more profound. There were no "old-timers" to visit on the Mountain at my dad's side, no dad. No cattle to chase or Clydesdales to pretend to harness. Now we had TV! Bathtubs and a Modernist, glass and steel constructed elementary school.

I grew up the 5th daughter to my dad and the 4th to my mother. Those ahead of me were all so interesting! One kept sharks in our bathtub for a science project. Another was always class president. First-born was a Political Science major. The last became a Wildlife Biologist. These minds surrounded me and challenged me. Our mother, a journalist, encouraged us to express our truest talents. I entered school on the young side, and along with my sisters, we became known as the Wallis Girls. The family mantra was always to do your best. In first grade, watching mom prepare food after work, she shook her wood spoon at me saying, "Barbie, you have to go to college! And I can't help you. You have to get scholarships!" I'd learned what college was, but, what was a scholarship? If ever I got a B, she would say, "You can do better." Luckily, I liked school. But I needed to get away from all of the energy, so beginning in elementary I'd go to my bedroom and draw. I'd copy everything. I taught myself the names of artists from mom's art history book. This study was my escape, and it allowed me to breathe.

My eldest sister worked the long night shift in a fish cannery to earn enough for college. I wished somehow to make it easier on her so I wrote to Michael Landon, who I read in TV magazine made a six-figured salary for his role as Little Joe. I asked him if he could help my sister go to college? I never did hear from him, but my sister made her way. I did my part and got many scholarships, including tuition for four years at the university of my choice in the state of Washington. It was a shock to find out that art was considered unworthy of the scholarship funds, and it was recommended I study law or architecture.

I spent two years in the Architecture program at a school far away. I wanted to get lost. I finished with a degree in Art, but in order to be funded I had to take micro- and macro- economics, business and law courses. While writing a Comparative Economics paper I wrote my philosophy on money. I decided I was a Socialist, but one combined with capitalism. I created Barbarism a way to redistribute the wealth. In this system, all talents were honored and funded to encourage creativity and excellence.

I was engaged to my kind, football player boyfriend. His family was well to do, and we were given a down payment on a house, a new car and more. But, as our wedding day approached toward the end of my 22nd year, I grew increasingly depressed. I didn't know why. Finally, I broke the engagement a few weeks before the wedding. I returned gifts. I apologized profusely. I wept. I didn't know where I was going. My father had me come to his ranch. He listened and told me it was okay.

A friend invited me to go backpacking in the Canadian Rockies. Carl and I rode the freight train at dusk from the Seattle yards to the Canadian border, where they had heard a couple of kids with back packs were stowed away. They let us cross the border at 3 am. Hitchhiking from Banff to Jasper we met Dennis. He picked us up. I rode in the back of the pickup with his 12-string guitar and dog, named Luke. We all camped together several days. The magnificent Rockies put on a stunning show! Dennis visited me in Seattle, where we explored the city. Then, I showed him my wilderness ranch. He chopped wood there and hiked with me into the thick forests. He said, "This is an incredibly beautiful place! But, it was your parents' dream and we all have to create our own." That struck me so true. Effortlessly, he said something I needed to hear. Everyday thereafter he wrote me letters. We moved to Los Angeles, so he could pursue acting, which fit well with my goal, to make art. This longhaired, handsome man, with a bowie knife strapped to his thigh was just right with me.

When we arrived in Los Angeles where his actor brother lived, we got jobs and lived together to save money and encourage each other. I'd hike to the top of Laurel Canyon and look out over the city and wonder how I would manage it all? We'd discuss ideas into the wee hours. They analyzed the arts of acting, directing and writing in ways I'd never seen. They were my interesting family. Early that first year, I had a dream that Dennis had taken me to Disneyland. We were too long in the park. When we got back to the main gate, it swung shut and we were locked into the Kingdom overnight. I remember being frightened, but then it happened, the artists, musicians and the actors came out, and the world was not strange anymore, instead, it was quite sublime.

Image specs. I KNOW WHERE I'M GOING; 37x37", oil in high-melt wax over constructed leach papers on canvas Udi Itzhayek Collection, Israel

www.barbarakerwin.com

Laurel Paley

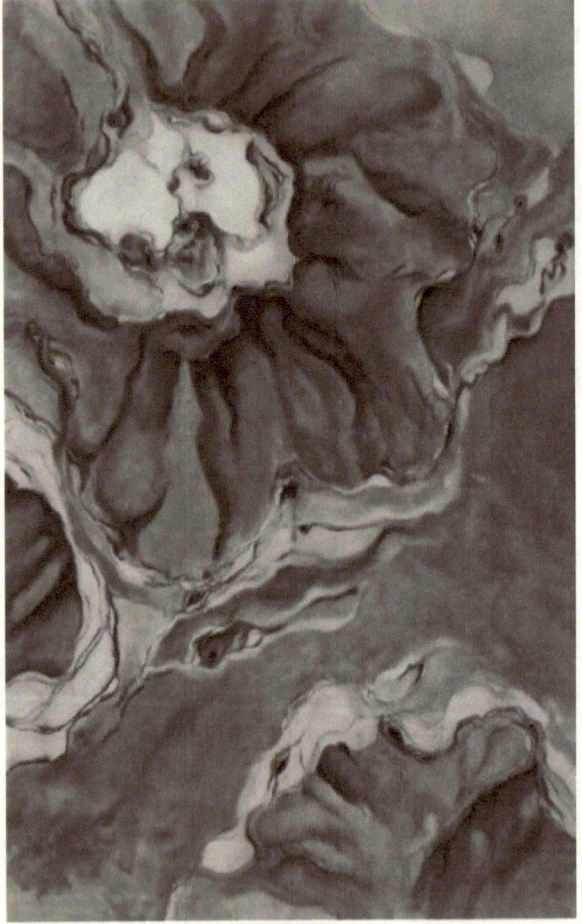

Appetite

It was early by Mexican standards, and it was hot.

I headed out first thing in the morning, stumbling alone along quiet dusty hilly streets. I was making my way to spend time with the dead, in a country in love with the dead, at a place made famous for its mummified dead.

Of course I have encountered the dead before, dead men whom I have dearly loved. A brother-in-law, a newly dead body, still in a hospital bed, waxy and turning a translucent gray-yellow-green, no longer inhabited, but carrying indications of recent residency. My father, already several days dead, lying clothed in a wooden box. I had only a few confused and jet-lagged moments before the box was closed, to be lowered and covered with dirt.

Both looked peaceful—but isn't that just my interpretation (or even wishful thinking)? Both brought me into a shocked sense of not knowing, not knowing anything, really not knowing much at all. Of course I grieved for them (and so many others, friends and colleagues, family members). But grief feels small, odd, plain, and insufficient.

I have drawers full of dried, dessicated dead things—flowers and petals, navels from navel oranges, mutant lemons, headless doll bodies and bodyless doll heads, found unidentified objects, animal skulls from the desert. I love these things. Many lead me into my drawings, photographs, paintings. I collect them, draw them, contemplate them, and watch them turn to dust.

I have held femurs and scapulae. I have prodded at human cadavers, breathing formaldehyde and wearing gloves/goggles/gear. I have talked directly about anatomy—blood, fat cells, muscles, and bones—to hundreds of Life Drawing students, watching them cringe at the thought of what lies under the skin. But what lies under the thought? What lies under breath? What I cannot—or cannot yet—or may never—know prods back at me.

Perhaps all this is what led me to Mexico. Perhaps this is why I wanted so badly to go to Guanajuato, to its museum full of ordinary people who were dead.

I made my way early, a couple days after the grand, raucous Día de los Muertos. The streets were mostly empty, a few dogs barked, a few cars passed. So many people warned me of crowds at the Museum of Mummies that I was the first person—the only person—in line when it opened.

The famous mummies of Guanajuato died during a cholera epidemic in the 1830s. They were disinterred (possibly to open up space in the cemetery, possibly because no one was left to pay their perpetual burial tax) and discovered to be more than just piles of anonymous-looking bones. Their bodies mummified naturally, some gracefully, some even "wearing" clothes that had only partially disintegrated. After years stacked in a municipal building (where viewers could pay a few pesos to look), many of the mummies now rest in glass cases, viewed by thousands in Guanajuato's Museo de las Momias.

I hurried there, camera in hand. I had to see.

I entered a cool, darkened museum, where the dead (and wall tags) were exposed and illuminated. They leaned in their glass cases, many with what seemed like facial expressions. At least one of them was known to have been buried alive accidentally, but several had facial expressions of terror, shock, and pain. (Do the dead somehow open their mouths after burial? Are the grimaces actual grimaces? Are they from the pain of dying?) I spent time with each, capturing images that would help me teach anatomy, capturing other images that captured me. Other than a couple museum guards and one other visitor, I was alone with the mummies and their silent screams.

At first it felt like an insult, photographing the mummies. How dare I take pictures of the final, intimate moments of these strangers, preserved by altitude and dry air? How dare I photograph their bodies, some no longer covered by garments or even a shroud? Who am I to wield a camera at the faceless, lifeless beings who nonetheless felt so alive? I apologized to them, and then began to ask them questions. "Did you die alone? Did you die in pain? Were you afraid? Were you angry?" "Were you already dead when they buried you? Did they make a horrific mistake?"

As I write this, I am laughing at myself. Of course I didn't believe that the mummies could hear me. Now, writing this, I also see that I addressed them in English, not Spanish.

I continued.

I couldn't stop looking at the mummies' gestures, their elegantly pointed toes (they died lying down, not standing up), their hands and arms cradling the air and themselves. Flesh dried and tightened; overweight bellies and large breasts deflated, flattened, dimpled, and folded. Some of the mummies had partially decomposed, their faces resembling Day of the Dead folk art skulls.

Even the mummified remains show the indignity of dying and being devoured by life itself. Sometimes flesh had torn away, revealing intricate batches of tendons and shrunken, skinny muscles. Sometimes flesh had tiny wormholes. Sometimes the skeletons were partly visible, but mostly what drew me was a sense of the confluence of life and death from the more fully preserved bodies, occasionally still clad in suits, boots, dresses, shifts.

So I stood in the cool, dark quiet, murmuring. I thanked the mummies for the pictures I took. I thanked them in advance for the lessons my students would learn from their bodies. I apologized for staring at them, and thanked them for allowing me to be with their death.

An hour passed, maybe two.

The museum began to fill with the voices and bodies of the living, and rooms began to crowd. My reverie lifted; my inquiries quieted. I revisited a few mummies to say my good-byes and went out into hot bright light.

Title: Appetite.
Media: Drawing & painting media on canvas.
Size: 56 x 36 inches
Year: 2016

http://www.laurelpaley.com

Linda Sue Price

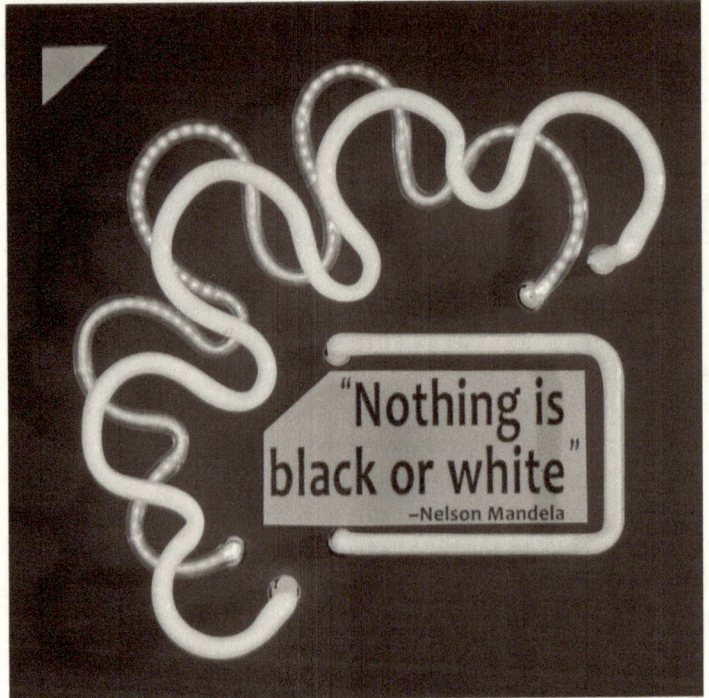

Nothing is Black or White

In my young adulthood I was in a mixed race relationship for almost ten years. Coming from an all white community that preached the golden rule it was stunning to experience white people from the other side. That was the beginning of my changing worldview. Every time we saw a cop we were pulled over. Fortunately nothing bad happened but it was always scary.

I started to understand nuance and began moving away from fixed points of view. I wrote poems about the shades of gray. I began saying nothing is black or white. Fixed positions, behaviors, rules, certainty and inflexibility became intolerable. I seized the opportunity to learn, grow, change and evolve. I learned about tolerance, acceptance and the joy of diversity.

I never developed a game plan for my life. I just tried to be engaged, learn as much as I could, do my best, take risks even when they were terrifying, have as much fun as possible and be flexible. A few of my favorite phrases that became guideposts—don't suffer for assholes, you are going to die whether you have fun or not so just have fun, staying in the moment is a discipline and practice, run from drama and change is the only constant.

From my perspective, I see people clinging to a fixed point of view that is causing them sadness and pain. For whatever reason, they can't let go and stay stuck. Suggesting they consider making a change and they just dig in and then wonder why they feel so bad. As the old phrase goes, doing the same thing over and over and expecting a different outcome is the definition of crazy. They want to think things are or can be black and white, which in reality isn't possible.

And the interesting thing, the older one gets the more things change. As a child looking at adults of all ages, I thought their lives were fixed. They went to work Monday through Friday from 7 a.m. to 4 p.m. They had dinner at 5:30 p.m., etc. But their lives were fraught with job insecurities, financial worries, and goals changed. My mom at age forty-five began studying to become an Enrolled Agent. This is the IRS equivalent to becoming a CPA. My father started cooking dinner because my mom was at college.

More recently I was reading an article about a person who translated ancient Chinese poetry. I was moved by the words he used to describe his work so I selected some of them to incorporate into my art. Part way through the art making I started remembering my own words and phrases. One of them was Nothing is black or white which it turned out was also said by Nelson Mandela.

At an exhibit, a psychologist saw the piece and said it would be perfect for her office because her clients want definitive black and white answers on how to live life. And no, she didn't buy the piece but I thought it was an interesting perspective on the phrase.

www.lindasueprice.com

Lorraine Bubar

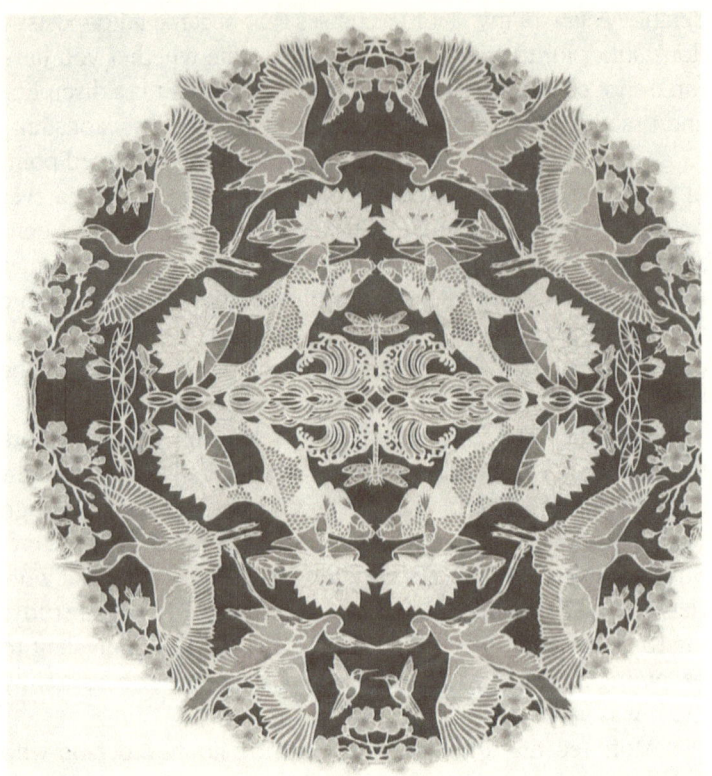

2016 seemed to be about trying to find a peaceful place in the world. Traveling far and wide, carefree and spontaneously as we did in our youth is not as possible. We are less innocent and naive. Close to home, with the increase in traffic, we are being forced to seek out what is in our own neighborhoods, to see what they have to offer so that we do not have to be endlessly stuck in our cars. My backyard has a koi pond and the peaceful sound of water and the calming rhythm of the koi swimming back and forth with dragon flies and hummingbirds circling is very peaceful. On a nice day, it is a peaceful retreat from the news and stress of living in an increasingly crowded city. Yet, danger lurks. A blue heron spotted our koi one day and remained a frequent, uninvited guest for weeks. This encounter inspired a series of mandalas that I cut out of paper to capture the hierarchy of species in my own backyard. The act of cutting my work at of paper is my mindfulness, where I lose myself, and forget about the city and the world swirling around me. My koi pond offers those same qualities. But, one species does prey upon the other. During 2016 I volunteered as a Super Citizen Scientist for the Natural History Museum of Los Angeles. I had no idea that Los Angeles, among other things, is a hotbed of biodiversity. On a regular basis, I recorded all of the insects that I found in my backyard. I had no idea that there was such variety, among the spiders, butterflies, bees, dragonflies, etc. I became aware how these species are seasonal, one month I had mud daubers and the next I had flame skimmers in vast numbers. So, my mandalas focused on the levels of prey, moving from the inner to the outer parameters. And I was only distracted when I had to run outside to startle the heron away so it did not prey on my koi. Peace disrupted!

www.lorrainebubar.com

Mara Thompson

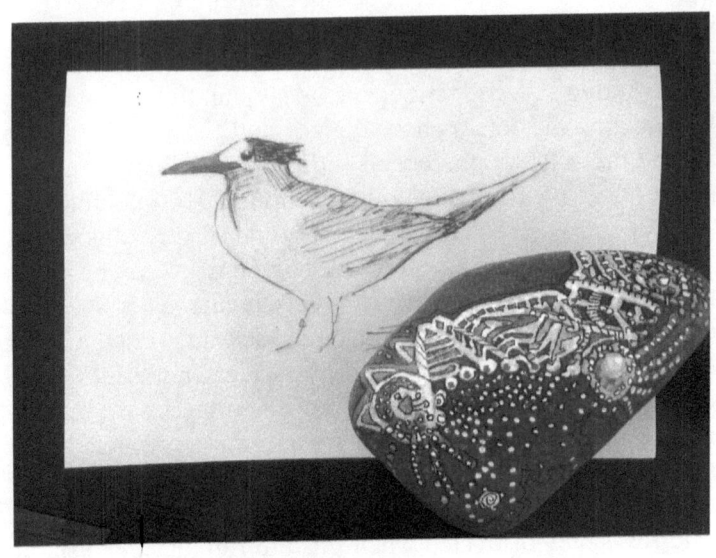

We agreed to meet at the Hammer Museum café on February 28, 2016. Ten former students and friends of artist and teacher Franklyn Liegel gathered to celebrate his life near the fourth anniversary, February 29th, of his unexpected death.

The exhibition, much like Franklyn, championed the experimental. *Leap Before You Look: Black Mountain College 1933 - 1957* contained works by a variety of the instructors and students. One of my all time favorites, Ray Johnson, was represented there, an artist whose collages Franklyn introduced me too. Ray was quirky just as Franklyn was. I loved both of their art making, their willingness and need to be themselves. We all figured that the *Leap Before You Look* exhibition would be "Franklyn approved"

Franklyn always encouraged experimentation in your art. He took great joy in the process and passed on that energy to his students. Somehow he was Special, a special teacher and friend. Unique some would say, others would say volatile.

One could not argue that many students would repeat his workshops again and again... and again, while others would leave and want their money back.

There was always something new to learn. He inspired us. After four years of him being gone many of his students still gather sans instructor to make art together, and join in memorials like the one in February 2016.

After his passing I, and each of his loyal students, were forced to become our own teachers. This proved to be a rough time for my art making. Yes, I could still hear his voice of encouragement and suggestions and I still had copious notes from his classes. Fortunately I had purchased a couple of his artworks while he was with us and they serve to remind me of his spirit. But still, not receiving the surprise phone call or the very occasional lunch together, being unable to attend his twice a year workshops with the same group of loyal students took its toll.

Around the same time period I became full up with exhibiting in certain art group venues. For seven years I entered juried shows two to three times a year, as I recall I only was rejected once. I won prizes, and sold a few. That avenue felt played out. Though I still belong to the group I no longer entered the opportunities.

I struggled with too many avenues of art interest. Collage, oils, fiber arts, subjects of exploration seemed a swirl. As the first summer after his death came my studio was hot more often than not. I stopped showing up.

The work required paring down the supplies and subject focus became larger and larger in my mind so I shut the door on it.

To alleviate the depression from being "artless" I added many outside walks, most of them along our seashore. Gleaning was always a possibility whether it was lost sand toys or removing garbage. Some days there would be lots of shells, some times lots of rocks. I began to use shells and rocks as surfaces to paint. The sand toys are still waiting for inspiration.

By 2016, the fourth year after his passing the funk began to lessen. I started in by choosing to work with a medium that

I had known my whole life. Sewing, all manner of embroidery and fiber arts felt like comfort food for me. Then I added in crochet (having been previously enthralled with The Reef Project). Slowly I am learning enough to be able to construct free form pieces without patterns.

Concurrent with that I picked up drawing again. It is compact and connects me to a place or a feeling.

2016 was the happy turning point in a four-year battle to get back to it. We soldier on, yes?

Not truly up to speed again I occasionally pine for a teacher like Franklyn who was supportive and quirky, funny and troublesome and always a surprise. I look for opportunities but so far, none have struck a spark. My website has not been updated in a while, but it does exist.

www.Mythmara.com

Mara Zaslove

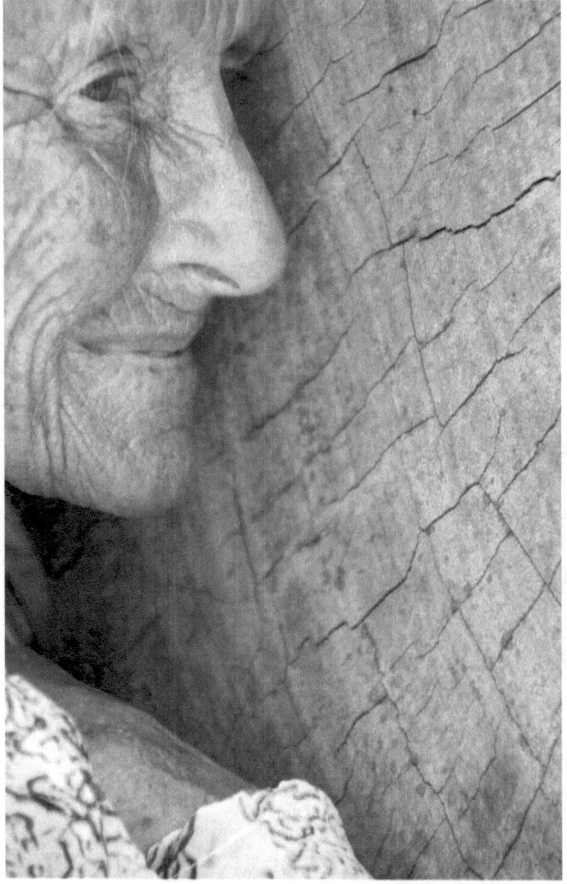

Inge Rekenye

Recently, I have been fortunate to become friends with a woman, a senior, who is lithe and has a zest for life. She has a dark tan contrasted with white hair and her creped skin appears taut and defined. She is comfortable within her body and herself and embraces each day with an adventurous spirit.

How I would love to be like her when I am 89!

I met her about 4 years ago while were both taking Chi Gong at Emeritus College. It was a multigenerational class and

I naturally gravitated toward her. We have become fast friends. A year or so ago, I approached her about the possibility of photographing her. She was totally open to the idea. Since then, we have met every few months and had a collaborative session. The locations have varied and it has been a wonderful way to enjoy each other's company. The more time spent together, the more we have gotten to know about each other.

She is originally from Germany and was in her teens during the war. She immigrated to Canada after college, became an LVN and within three months of settling there, she met her future husband. He was from Budapest, Hungary and they moved to Los Angeles so that he could go to art school. After years as an art director in advertising in Providence, Detroit, New York and Los Angeles, they opened up an equestrian store in Palos Verdes. They brought horses over from Germany and supplied their needs to participate in the Olympics.

In her mid-seventies, she rowed 33 miles to Catalina with her outrigger team. After 53 years of marriage, her husband passed away. She has since continued enjoying her life by keeping both mentally and physically alert. She has strong and loving relationships and is always looking ahead.

As our lives move on, it becomes difficult to keep everything on track approaching the final station. Inge Rekenye's grace, dignity and exuberance in life should be examples for us all.

In our youth-oriented society, someone like her, those older/elderly, are often dismissed and treated as if they were invisible. As much as the environment is in the political forefront, aging and all that embodies this "closer to the end of life" transition is not a hot topic. It seems critical that we start valuing the older generation and issues that confront them and heighten our awareness and embrace this population as a critical resource. This is especially poignant since the 'baby boomer generation' is moving towards this chapter in masse.

Fear of the unknown often distances one's desire to learn. My friendship with this woman has whetted my appetite about the aging process and the opportunities that accompany it. Becoming familiar with someone else's life story enhances one's appreciation of the passage of time since it encourages reflection of your own continuing journey.

This "free spirit" is documented by my imagery. I look forward to sharing many more years of friendship with her, and I hope to mirror her attitude both physically and mentally, as she and I travel down this inevitable path of aging.

www.marazaslove.com

Martin Cox

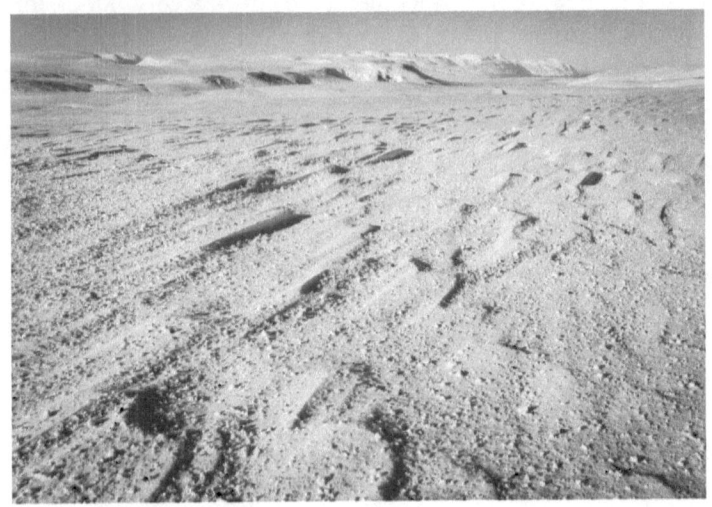

August was running out and the overnight temperatures in un-air conditioned LA were peaking. Unable to sleep I stumbled onto a website for art residencies.

Reading the text, I noticed that the application deadline was the next day. No time was given, or did tomorrow mean it was already passed as today in Iceland was over? I had no answers but decided to stay up all night and hammer out a proposal. In the early hours of what could be deadline day and dripping over the key board, I completed it and sent it off. My fear of the cold was overruled by the idea of heading to a tiny art residency in remote north-east Iceland.

That was late August 2015 in sticky Echo Park. While I lived without air conditioning, I usually did OK except for those few last fiendish days of the summer blast from which there is no escape.

I had exhibited a major project at the beginning of that year, I had hoped for more, maybe a book, a show or two out of it, but while there had been quite a lot of verbal interest little else was happening. My artistic practice felt a bit thin and slow. Thinking about a next project, I assumed I was heading towards another costly exhibition.

The idea of a residency was new to me, and refreshing. It seemed a great way to make work react to new landscape and think new thoughts. In September, I got an email from the Sam from the Iceland residency informing me that I had been selected to join with five artists for one month, and would I please arrive in Husavik, a small town in Iceland on February 15, 2016.

At first I was shocked by what I had done, and wondered if I should really go. It seemed like jumping in to a cold sea at night. What would I do there? Who would be there? Wouldn't it be too cold to be outside? Too dark to take photos? Was this a colossal wild goose chase? An Icelandic red herring? An Arctic fox?

I began some research and held a studio fundraiser on my birthday, fellow artists and friends bought my photographs in a salon style sale, now I had the option to go. What seemed a midnight whim was becoming a plan. I borrowed a huge coat, bought many layered high-tech garments from a hiking store and found massive snow boots. I gathered a few cameras and planned strategies incase I was locked in a bunker with the artic wind howling for days outside.

I set off a few days early so I could experience something of the capital Reykjavik before travelling on to the small northerly town.

On the wintry bus ride through deep snow I realized my fellow passenger was also heading for the same residency, a quick bond was made. Upon arriving in Husavik we met an Australian artist who was about to board and head back home after his residency. We had a five minute to exchange of information, though mostly it was for us to learn useful facts about characters of the town, how to get about, who to get rides from, where the secret hot tub was.

Once at the house, the three other artists appeared, we were gathered from Hamburg, Delhi, Bulgaria by way of Montreal, Oregon and me a British man living in Los Angeles. Our first meal together, a communal affair broke the ice and friendships were fast as a massive storm descended around the house with layers of snow piling at the door. Previous artist resident Emmi Jormalainen of Finland had left a stylish drawing of the town that served as a map to all that we needed. Art residencies are very varied, but the simple fact of leaving the familiar, living with people you would not otherwise meet, forging new friendships and thrusting yourself in to an entirely landscape and work mode I found to be entirely invigorating.

I met a sea Captain who worked in the harbor, a sociable man who became a friend, was keen to show the new arrivals some of the splendor of winter in Iceland. One bright searingly cold day he and I drove south toward Lake Myvtn along the less traveled gravel road.

The road took us far from any other living soul and rose up across a vast beautiful snow blasted plateau known as the Black Desert due to its dark lava soil, the farther we drove the emptier, whiter and more silent the land became. I was enthralled by the mood of the landscape, the vastness, the light. It was the same thrill and terror I had experienced when I first crossed the vastness of the USA as a young man in my 20s. I asked Vidir to stop the car, I had to get out and see all this, the wind had stopped, the sky was clear. Standing in the ecstatic vastness I started to take photographs in the freezing air.

This photograph reminds me that small specific actions can change your whole life and bring you to an entirely new horizon. It is always good to follow those coincidences. Mine life may never be the same as it was on that hot night in my Los Angeles studio, as I now prepare to depart Los Angeles once more to Iceland, a year later, embarking on my first solo museum show and new photographic projects on landscape.

www.martincox.com

Melissa Ann Lambert

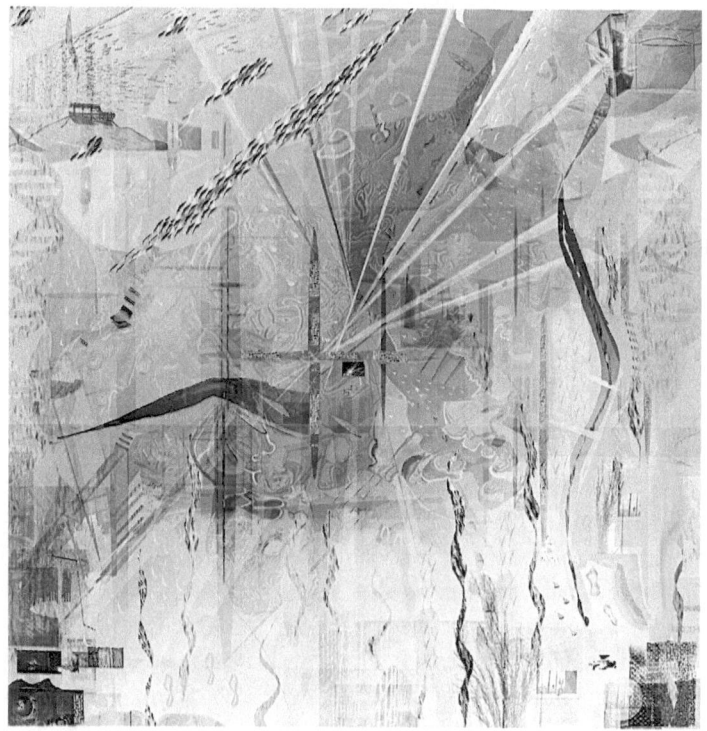

Tep Pyung Jung

I was in a very emotional place when I did this piece, thinking about my father, in particular, the the vacations we had – places like Big Bear, Big Sur, the Grand Canyon, the desert, Arrowhead, Apple Valley, this list feels endless.

And the motorcycle trip took - riding in the desert which is now considered politically incorrect but back then who knew? And that experience on the developing brain definitely lead to motor skill and reaction time development, and the ability to make snap decisions. So many amazing memories camping, chasing balsa wood airplanes in the desert, taking long hikes in the forest, staring up at the stars at night, watching meteors, campfires at the beach,... etc.

When my father passed, I felt a need do a piece with him in mind. Most of the symbology in this piece is highly personal, I wouldn't expect anyone to experience it or enjoy it in the same way that I do. For instance I see a station wagon in the upper left-hand corner, and that's what he drove us in. And his ashes are in the ocean off Dana point, so seaweed had to be included.

It was important to me that the color green was predominant, not just any green but a bright green – the color of leaves and grass and chlorophyll, because thinking of my dad is synonymous with the outdoors – feeling the wind on my face, experiencing the smells and textures and sounds and the beauty of nature with my family.

My father's grandfather was a sculptor, and my mother's father was an artist. Recognizing at an early age my talent however was supported on a limited basis (my father later apologized for this) because being an artist - at least on my fathers side - was equated with being flaky and poor. My fathers apology meant the world to me.

My father was also very influential in terms of my imagination. When I was little I would see things in marble floors and clouds. He said that when he was little he had a rich imagination too but that "we lose it as we get older." From that moment on I was determined never to lose my imagination. I exercised it every day while listening to classical music and imagining dancers in the air. My imagination has since become much stronger than when a child. And years later I was 'diagnosed' by a neuroscientist with synesthesia. Which means when I hear something I also see it, taste it, smell it, feel it. Yes, I dropped acid in my early 20's. There is no difference between my brain on acid or my brain off acid.

My dad also inspired in me a love of science. Lately I have been reading "The Holographic Universe" by Michael Talbot. This is what I wrote about one of my pieces that deals with the theme of holograms:

"My brain, which resembles a Jellyfish, is situated in the night sky. My eyes spew DNA like code into a spiral galaxy. A butterfly floats serenely toward "The Hologram."

We've evolved from a worldview containing closed systems and boundaries, reflective of a reductive dualism/linearity and imposing a contiguous range of naturally occurring phenomena. New intersections between art and science manifest as serendipitous resonance between artists and scientists exploring complex systems.

Holonomic brain theory, quantum physics, chaos theory, the butterfly effect, etc. have come to show the implicate order, explaining that space and time are no longer dominant factors in determining relationships. Each element in a hologram contains information about the whole, as the whole contains information about each piece. Our amazing brains are holograms.

http://MelissaAnnLambert.com

Michelle D. Ferrera

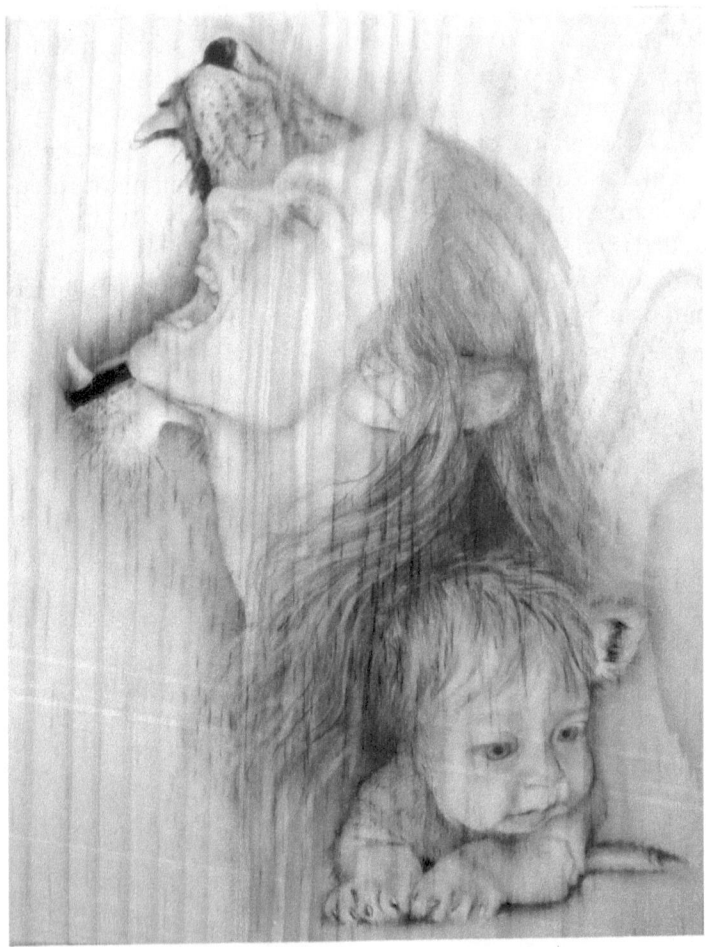

Pride & Joy

Being a first time mom, like so many others before me, is a constant balancing act…show them the world and its beauty, shield them from the evils, allow them freedom to become who they want to be without them hurting themselves, catch them when they fall…and of course bathe them, feed them, and the day to day responsibilities, all the while maintaining our own strength and individuality as women, not just moms, so they see for themselves how important it is to love yourself first and foremost. Maintaining full-time Artist as my other title this first year of her life has been one of the most challenging but incredibly full experiences I could have ever imagined, no matter how many people told me I'd feel like this. You only know when you experience it for yourself and everyone's experiences are different. I see her grow and become more every day, but I also see myself grow with her and also individually. I've never been more myself, strong, courageous, sensitive, patient, giving and all I want to do is record these moments and everything in between. I can't get over the amount of ideas, even at my most tired! It's this incredible force that I can't control, nor want to. As I've learned from a lifetime of rejection and loss, ride the great waves when they come. This has been a nonstop one. Though there are days I can't seem to think straight, beyond exhausted, can't feel my feet by days end, finish a piece that I'm not sure if I'll ever have another idea again...and then bam! Like that the little waves of ideas come, rejuvenating and motivating. And then I put my lil one, a future woman of the world, in her carrier, walk into Home Depot, sniff the fresh cut wood, smile a little, feel her wiggle on my back, and off my brain goes on another adventure of ideas her in tow. I will continue to capture my life, her life, and the lives around me because even with all the responsibilities and life that may sometimes get in the way combined with the exhaustion, I can't, NOT, create. And having my lil' cub beside me, watching her make her way towards her crayons and the way she correctly holds them and colors in a trance, much like myself as a child, I know no matter what she decides to do in her life, I will always support, love and protect her, for she is my Pride & Joy, my true legacy.

www.MDFerrera.com

Milo Reice

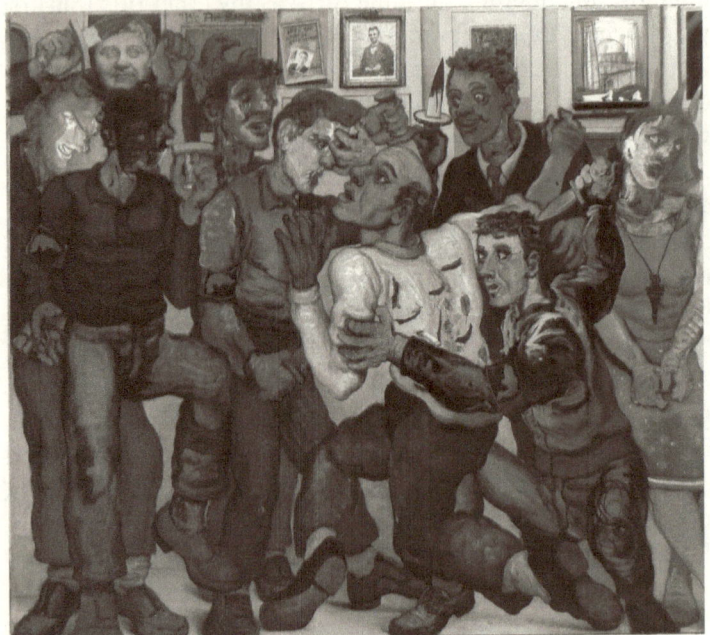

The Assassination of The American Soul (or the gutting of Julius Caesar by Brutus the Coward and his Coterie)- a diatribe aimed at trump

Trumpets for Caesar none for 45.

I was a huge Baseball fan once- a type of fan who'd video tape a game- and after ignoring newspaper kiosks - on returning home I'd watch the full game. in 1986 lucky to attend game six of the World Series, it was Christmas day's equivalent of joy, the high-point of my life as a fan. But as The Chinese say to convey perfection there must be a flaw some- where within?!

Taking out the politics of "Bread and Circus", the cama- raderie, the openly unabashed joy across all classes of people is what I have not forgotten, -it was democracy expressed won- derfully, The Tower of Babel reversed- as strangers, different nationalities managed conversation which just minutes before on the subway or on the streets wouldn't accomplish. If I were an ancient, seated in the Flavian Colosseum I would, given an ancient mindset, be enthralled just like at Shea Stadium gazing at the beautiful expanse of green, espying the architecture- I'd gaze down at the gold dusted sand, the marble stairwells, the hundreds of statuary, and I'd be reveling in the joyous abandon about me.

But then trumpets would sound and we'd all shift gazes to the royal box to Hail Caeser- why not? - Vespasian and Titus were by all accounts good guys. So I'd cheer.

But in Queens the organ sounding periodically wasn't for any Caesar that I recall- for who or which celebrity or politico, "the bells tolled" I only recall but one couple. Of them, one I sort of liked via a disinterested factoid/tabloid,eyewitness news way, however her partner I rather disliked - a counterfeit Trimalchio he was , less likable than the original- I saw no decency, no ethics of value, only bravado and ego. It was this half of the couple I'd compare to the young Domitian, Vespasian's youngest and future psychotic emperor I'd not be wanting to hail.

Vespasian looked like Lyndon Johnson, and Titus had "it" so to speak. "Charisma" for its myriad inexplicable ways consistently contradictory from one anointing to the next is a hard thing to figure or predict so when organ its arpeggios complete I looked downwards the rows to the grinder's serenaded celebrated couple. Wealthily well dressed, and in her case smiling genuinely, they seemed illuminated in technicolor tinged with a touch of sulphuric yellow. But I was a Mets fan not their fan so for many years they were to my memory of game #6's majesty and spectacle, of "Mookie" and company, of Billy Buckner, a mere footnote remembered with a little less than a smirk. Rome's Horace or Juvenal would have found in them perfect fodder for satirizing society and if I were there then, the perfect Plebeian useful for their P.O.V.

Now, I'd always wanted to make an assassination painting, preferably fictive one as archetype rather than a specific one but as an American I felt it'd have to be Lincoln's. Alas I never got to it. In 2015 I began a series of studies for paintings of

Ceasar and Cleopatra and so It happened that I did a few of his assassination!

On November 13, 2016 one dark day of the few after election day I finally began my vitriolic Assassination of The American Soul…; piggy banked upon the subject of Caesar's death I poured my anger- I did not want to bloviate verbally as everyone around me but to mourn, to leave a visual testament. Without the space here to elaborate, I am of the opinion that Caesar was for his world a liberal democrat, brilliant statesman and modern man of his time, attuned to the needs of his day, careful of bad repercussions- certainly no troglodyte. Depicting his death by a horde of self righteous, lying, two-faced politicians, out for themselves really, I sought to convey the horror (by implication) of what was lost, and what could have been had Caesar lived.

Now life's funny, who knows what one will come to do in the future? Back in 1986 in Shea Stadium happy but for the momentary distracting "apotheosis" of the celebrated couple in the boxes below I might have resembled Romans who'd gladly cheered his father and brother but later wanted to cat-call Domitian or laugh in scorn, or perhaps hide . Though I'd essentially brushed the more vulgar half of the couple, the man, from my mind it would've been impossible then to conceive that 31 years later he'd be the provocation for my painted diatribe.

Do The Chinese also say: to achieve terribleness there must be a mote of perfection - of beauty within?- then at least I painted a work that honors my country's better aspects, despite the painting's genesis rooted in the loathsome electoral outcome of 2016.

As for #45 I only wish 45 was a monogram on his belly button protecting ties not the designation of his undeserved position- And I am not talking Baseball positions.

Julius Caesar I salute you! Lincoln and Barack too!

www.miloreice.com

Peter Hess

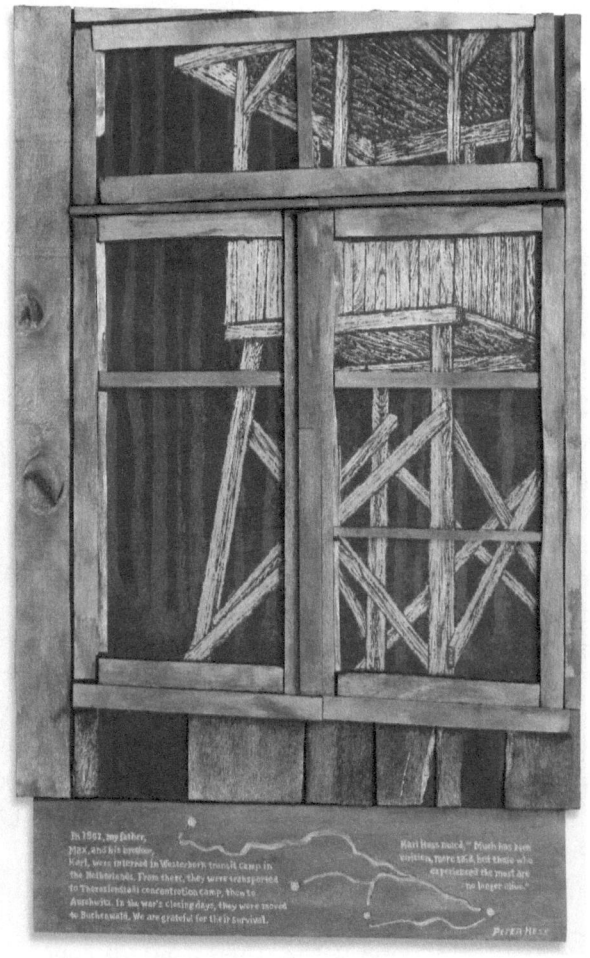

Being a "glass half empty" kind of guy, I struggled to come up with a subject when I was invited by artist/curator Raoul De la Sota to create an Ex-Voto piece for inclusion in his 2016 exhibition, "Silent Testimonies," at L.A.'s Avenue 50 Studio. As Mr. De la Sota explained it in an email, "Ex-Votos are actually "gifts," a gratitude of thanks given to a deity or any other person or object that helped to create a "miracle" or saved a life, gave one good fortune, recovering from an illness, escaping a near-death experience or simply solving a difficult situation."

While happy for the opportunity to participate, it presented a discomfiting challenge. No subject readily sprang to mind. Nothing, at least, of sufficient gravity. It isn't that I'm ungrateful. I'm just not the demonstrative sort. The work I do is more likely to deal with social or cultural commentary or art historical references. A picture's formal qualities are usually my first consideration. If personal or biographical elements make an appearance, they are typically cloaked. I don't like my work to be about me. Compounding the dilemma was my lack of belief in a deity on which to confer my gratitude.

The answer, I decided, would be to put a sharper point on the work that was currently occupying me. I'm engaged in paintings and prints I call "woodworks." Lumber forms — planks, boards, timbers, etc. — are practically the only element represented in these pieces. They depict once-living things, extinguished and pressed into a second life of utilitarian service. In their arrangements of walls and towers, some of these works allude to oppression or suggest alienation.

I made a decision to re-imagine one of my tower images, making it specifically about my father's experience as a young Jewish man interned in concentration camps during World War II. I crafted a new version of a tower image in wood and paint, and appended a plaque with a carved statement. It reads, in part:

"In 1942, my father, Max, and his brother, Karl, were interned in Westerbork transit camp in the Netherlands. From there, they were transported to Theresienstadt concentration camp, then to Auschwitz. In the war's closing days, they were moved to Buchenwald. We are grateful for their survival."

It came out nicely, and ended up being selected as the image for the show's announcement card. While I was pleased to have completed an arguably appropriate answer to the challenge, it left me in something of an existential quandary.

In my most cynical moments, the epic rants of the Austrian writer, Thomas Bernhard, resonate with me. Notably the ones in which he charges his parents with committing two crimes against him. First, by procreating him; second, by raising him. I have felt like that. Parents so often seem to feel that they are owed congratulations for conferring life on their offspring, and that their children never sufficiently appreciate the selfless sacrifice their progenitors made by adding them to the nearly 8 billion already occupying the planet, then putting food in their mouths. I think this parental attitude is nonsensical. Children come into being for all kinds of reasons. Mainly selfish ones. I seriously doubt that the notion of bestowing the gift of life on future generations is high on the list. No child asks to be born. Are parents owed gratitude?

And yet, by expressing gratitude for the survival of my father, am I not at the same time acknowledging thankfulness for my own existence? After all, if Max Hess had suffered the same fate of extinction during his horrific internment as had the majority of his family members, I (and my brothers and sister) would never have been born. Without him, there would be no me.

That is something I had never thought about before. About existence, sure. But never from this perspective. For a moment, I empathized with Jimmy Stewart's character, George Bailey, in the Frank Capra classic, "It's A Wonderful Life." In the film, George is afforded a glimpse of a world into which he was never born.

So, am I grateful for my father's survival and—by extension—my own existence?

I remain grateful for his survival.

www.PeterHessArt.com

Ron Therrio

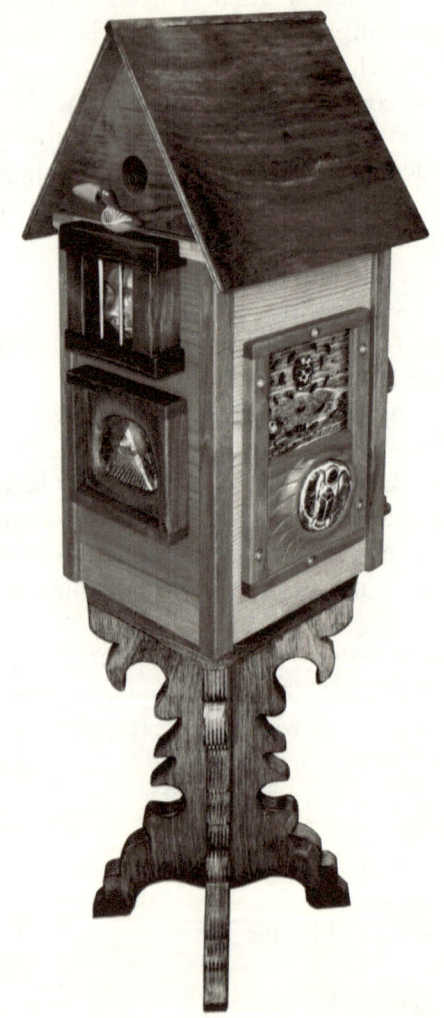

"There's no place like home" This work involved an internal dialog on how some people as adults may work to overcome deep emotional damage from childhood and the fact that not all homes are safe (or feel safe) for the children that inhabit them, whether it be due to unstable parenting, a sibling that bullies or even geo political instability. Using old pieces of wood including some from the dismantled bookshelves of the now defunked Either Or Bookstore in Hermosa Beach CA., many of the figurative elements are castings from projects I had sculpted in the past and a few are found objects.

The work resembles a tall bird house of sorts on a pedestal. When the roof is removed. you can see the interior diorama has only a ladder to descend into the dark space and a scary monster waiting down below, the monster is vague, represented as a geometric shape with only a large gapping mouth full of very sharp teeth. Outside in the front, the house has two main elements, a young face behind bars with a bird perched above him almost taunting him and below that, a panel with the pyramid topped with the all-seeing eye. The hinged pyramid panel opens to expose a portal to within, symbolizing control by an ultimate authority or the perception of power beyond one's control. To the right on the side panel is a panel with two elements, above a depiction of the internal emotional turmoil created within a world of fear or threat real or maybe only perceived, below this in the lower half is a relief of the Egyptian Scarab holding a Sun Disc to ward off evil and ensure a safe journey. This panel has a secret component, it can be raised carefully and with focus gently held in place by magnets to reveal a glass dome with the Chinese caricature of longevity painted on it, symbolizing the amount of time sometimes needed to transcend one's past. Moving around to the back panel, it too also has two elements, the first being a window of stained glass for clarity (or lack of) to within one's self & the other is a Nome'ish sentry, reminding one to stay present & ever vigilant. The last panel features the winged Moai which to me symbolizes a degree of enlightenment, next to him, just below is the Crow and he is the trickster. The Crow is hiding a secret compartment that reveals a brass coin the coin is inscribed with the words "NO CASH VALUE" too remind us "all that glitters is not gold". To say it another way and maybe more clearly, what we may perceive to be tragic or hurtful in the moment of our experiencing can indeed be emotionally crippling, or it can be the thing that triggers us to uncover new strengths or a chance to develop new coping skills. I am not saying this is always the case, this is just a reflection of my own experience and my thought journey while creating this piece and I found for me this can occur only when (and if) I am able to view things from a new and unfamiliar perspective.

www.rontherrio.com

Scott A. Trimble

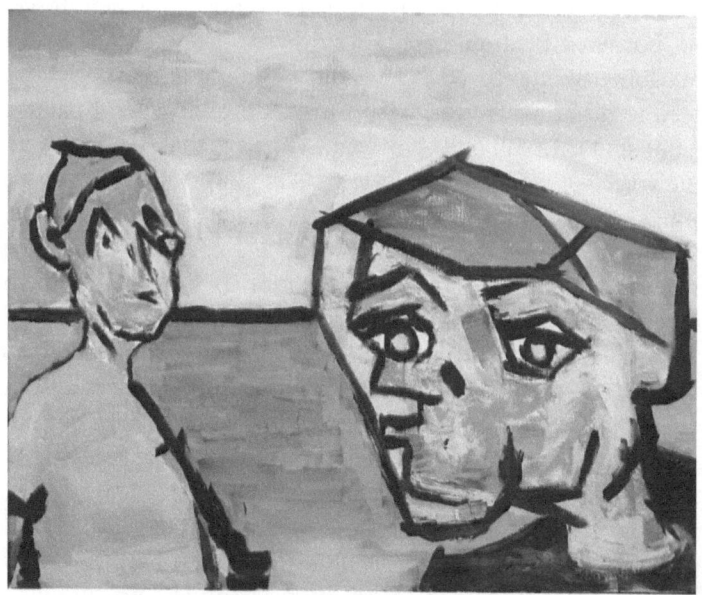

They knew just as everyone know

The doc-O

Despite all the horrible changes wrought by 2016, despite the world's headlong plunge into insanity, I remain forward-thinking and forward-looking; in other words, more than ever I am still focused on the doc-O.

The doc-O is an auto-biographical mocumentary, an auto-mocumentary Penny says is not really about me, but about *her*. Women should always be the focus of any story any way. They are far more interesting than men, more complex, more detail-oriented, more beautiful, of course, better protagonists in every way. But the doc-O is not *really* about Penny. It is really about me, but the dead me, not the living me. So that's why I can't tell the story – I will be dead when the film is made. So Penny must be the narrator. In that sense, the doc-O is definitely about Penny.

What appeals most about painting is that I get to do whatever I want. Let me say that again: *whatever I want.* When I am not painting, people love to tell me not just where to get off, but what I can do on my way there. They tell me what I am doing wrong, or what I should be doing and even what I need to do or, worse yet, what I must do. But when I paint, I get to shut them all out. The beauty of art is that it comes from one voice – it is *the creator's own point of view.* That is how I see things: (1) Lies appeal to no one. (2) Beauty is truth laid bare. *Your* truth must come only from *you.* If someone else joins in the creative process, it's a collaboration (which has its own appeal). It is not thoroughly unique. And in my case, it would make painting like everything else: me doing someone else's bidding. I listen to advice and opinions, but block it all out when I am painting, for the sake of the work. I block it out gleefully. I enjoy turning my mind off and just playing with oil paints. *The thicker the better.*

The original premise of the doc-O is this: a very beloved artist dies, leaving behind an amazing body of work, and a filmmaking crew rushes to his home to interview surviving family members about this illustrious aesthetic giant, this visionary whose mere thoughts had changed so much in such a short amount of time. Everything about him was monumental, and the filmmakers regard the painter as nothing short of epic. To their chagrin, the painter's family thought he was a bit of a goofball. They were amused by him (he loved to make them laugh), but they neither understood nor appreciated his true genius. Thus, the filmmakers expected bountiful insights into his painting and the intense psychology behind it, but only got shaggy-dog stories about their dear departed former resident kook.

I realized there aren't enough shaggy-dog stories about this resident kook to prop up two hours of viewing time, or even ninety minutes. So the great humbling of 2016 was the realization that the doc-O would need to be transformed into something slightly more doable, something that could carry an audience's interest for long enough. And we found the answer:

the doc-O will consist of two main parts: (1) the introduction, which simply states that the film is about a now dead but still beloved painter; and (2) the rest of the doc-O, which will be a series of perfect endings for the doc-O. Pretty much every day in 2016 I have written a fresh ending for the doc-O. For me personally, the ending is the most important part. It's the part where my lover sums me up, tells the world what made me special to her; what made me *me*. I don't want to give away all of those great endings yet, but I'll tell you a couple. Well, I'll tell you one, at least. Here's one of the endings: Penny remembers the time she answered the phone and it was one of my "groupies," some young girl asking to speak with me. Penny says hello and the groupie asks whether Scotty is there. Penny has never called me Scotty. I can only think of five people who have ever called me Scotty: Judi, Else, Traci, Karen and Michelle (who was my very first groupie). So maybe it makes sense that the groupie called me Scotty, but Penny long ago vowed to never call me Scotty. Yet in this instance, she could not resist: she howls down the long hallway of our painter-funded big house *Scotty! Phone call!!!*. In this particular ending of the doc-O Penny retells this story, then she tells the film-maker, quite proudly, "I NEVER called him Scotty. Never!," to which the filmmaker quietly responds, "You just did."

There are lots and lots and lots more endings to the doc-O, so please don't worry. *You will be sated at the end of the doc-O.* We will pick out the best of the best of the great endings and end it with that one.

In the meantime, it's now 2017. I wasn't ready for it, but a new year came and, with it, 2016 passed into history. And so will 2017. And so will I. Which is why I need to make the doc-O. I need evidence to remain that I was here. I need to add my two cents' worth to the ongoing conversation about art. Because I want to. Not because Penny wants me to, or tells me to. I want to do the doc-O because it makes Penny laugh. The idea of it and our nightly talks about it make us both laugh. That is how we spent 2016. That is why despite all the craziness of 2016, including some of the nuttiest, most inane ideas you've ever heard, despite the stifling stupidity, I remain looking forward and thinking ahead. In other words, more than ever I am still focused on the doc-O.

: http://www.facebook.com/scott_trimble.54

Sharon Suhovy

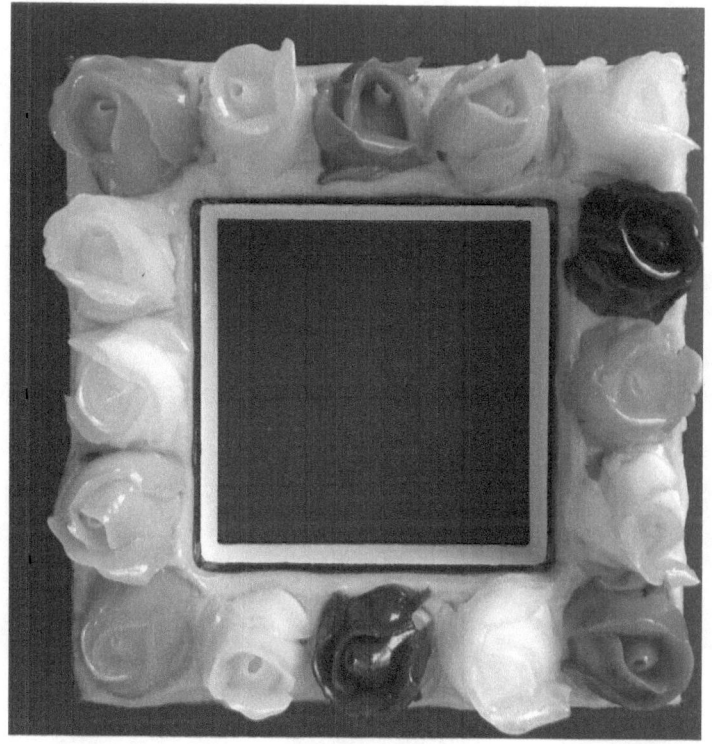

Vandermeiden

It was the month of May, on a Saturday.

The morning was flaunting a "New Moon", and it was my Birthday. May 7.

My birthday being so close to Mother's Day, has always been a combined event.

I was actually born at 11:59pm… so, Mother's Day falling on May 8, this year, made it a perfect weekend to celebrate them together.

My children took me to Las Vegas. We went to a show, and an amazing dinner. They're all educated, hard-working, generous, humorous, and compassionate people. I love them deeply.

But as I sat there eating dinner, I missed my mother. I wished she could have known my children as adults. I was 32 when she passed at age 53.

Now, I was turning 65.

I will remember May 7 as the day I realized that all of my children were grown adults, living in their own homes, married with children, running their own businesses, responsible for other people, and having warm compassionate souls, treating their mom to a birthday of a lifetime. They gave me their time.

I think that turning 65 was a really check/shock. There is no going back. I became very aware of my mortality. My health. My concept of time. My abilities. My inabilities.

May 7, 2016 was a tipping point. It was a rite-of-passage too.

I applied for Medicare!

www.facebook.com/pages/SharonSuhovy/157946574216476

Simone Gad

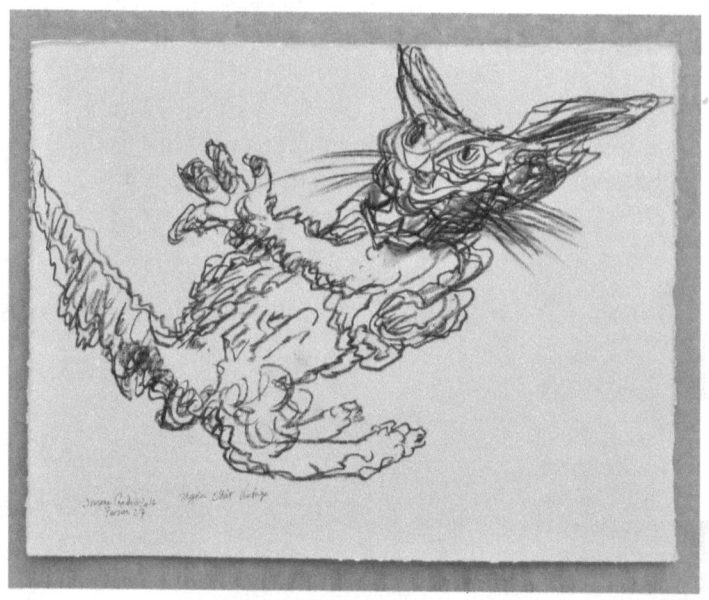

Mignon Chat Vintage Sur Papier

My parents aunt and uncle hated pets-especially cats and I wasn't allowed to have one when I was a child and teenager living at home. They were holocaust survivors of Poland filled with dread so the idea of having an animal around in their apartment was a complete and utter threat to them. For me it was constant sadness as I was groomed for show-biz at a very early age and my taking care of a pet was a constant threat to my mother-just the idea let alone the actually of my caring for something/someone else. My younger brother was not allowed a pet either. Later in life, I've had several cats adoring each and every one of them starting in 1972 when a high-school friend brought me Nathaniel-my very first kitty. Natie lived to be 15-sadly he was killed by a coyote when my then partner and I lived in Los

Feliz a block south of the boulevard. He was an indoor/out-door cat and I was not savy to the fact that kittykats live longer lives indoors solely. My animal rescue drawings I made in 2016 for my solo exhibition in New York City are hommages to these wonderful sentient beings. Ashes is my current kitty-last year in 2016 she became age 17.

http://www.ifac-arts.com/exhibitions/present-exhibitions/simone-gad-animal-rescue-drawings.html

Skye Amber Sweet

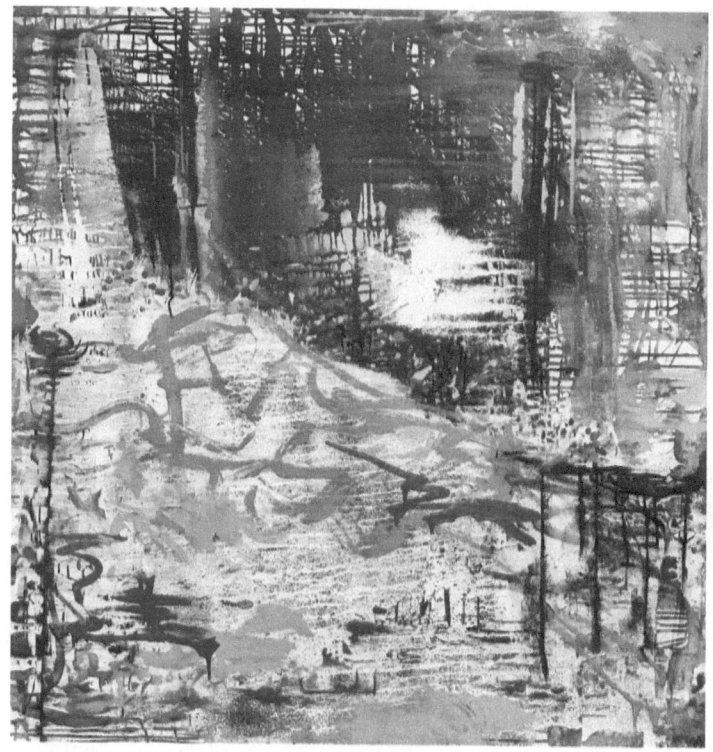

A Path To Somewhere

My initial thoughts behind the music playing in the background were overwhelming yet subtle. I felt loss this day in 2016 in the company of August and the emotion of sadness grew within my heart. With any discomfort of the heart, it helps me as an artist and creator to mastermind a piece that signifies enough emotion that runs deep through my soul while releases enough to comfort me upon completion. "The Path to Somewhere" is currently my favorite piece of art I have yet to have created in the five years as a full time artist.

I had moved to Los Angeles a few years back after starting my art career in Newport Beach where I started a company called Skyepoet in 2007. I had not used it to my ability until 2012 when I was laid off and became a full time artist. The day I painted this piece of art I felt as though my hard work and successes as an artist were put on hold in the new city unaccepting of my positivity and light. I felt as though Los Angeles and the artist communities were not about sharing love for art but wanted to be the spotlight so much as to degrade other artists. I had artists send me messages about what I do wrong as an artist and what my worth was. It stung because I truly wanted to help others, be creative and share love within the four walls of my canvases. Behind the closed doors, I knew my worth and why I paint and donate murals but felt if I did not follow the guidelines and rules in the art world I would continue to be disrespected and looked down upon.

I painted this piece "The Path to Somewhere" to signify that my path could be my own and any way that I chose. I decided to stop showing at galleries and went on a six-month hiatus to find my old path that had made me happy...the love for art and creation. I decided that within letting my emotions out in this piece, I would receive my freedom back as an artist enjoying rather than trying to keep up with associations, gallery event and other artists. I didn't want to feel as if I had to morph my beliefs and standards to impress other people whether a juror, curator, art critic.

I remember taking my forty eight by forty eight inch canvas and laying it flat on my art table. I turned on my music, mostly Neal Young and Leonard Cohen sipping my wine and pressing my fingers to the gesso letting all frustration and irritation out. I chose beautiful colors whose hues danced upon my fingers as I hand painted. I used no brushes proving to only enhance my freedom buy not sticking to any techniques. Being able to paint with purely emotional senses without though released me into my new path where my happiness shone through. This painting gave me the sense of self again and it was a path to somewhere instead of a dead end. I learned through painting it that I can overcome anything and anyone and the only one that I will ever try to impress again is myself.

There is a path within us all. The path we intend sometimes becomes a memory only creating a new one that takes us where we are supposed to go. The path to somewhere is better than a path to nowhere and if it's anywhere, I am happy to go. The path however will be my own.

"A Path To Somewhere" - Acrylic & Spray Paint - 48x48 - 2016 - $6,800

http://www.skyepoet.com

Susan Lizotte

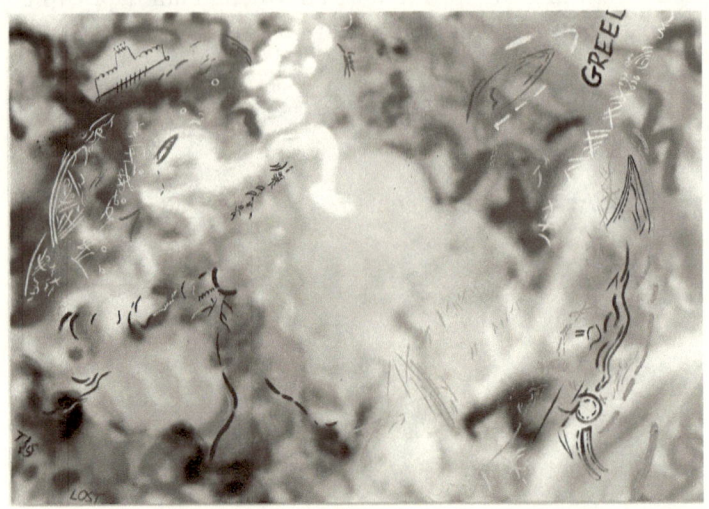

WhatYouCantSee

I painted *"What You Can't See"* over four months in the Spring of 2016 after reading (and being inspired by) Pascal Cotte's newest book "Lumiere On The Mona Lisa: Hidden Portraits". I devoured this book and still am obsessed. After more than a decade of studying the Mona Lisa with a multi spectral camera, Cotte has mapped layers and layers of paint under the now familiar surface, which now shows several other versions underneath the current painting. The portrait version of a young woman looking off to the side is particularly poignant for me. I have been completely fascinated by this intersection of science and art. Cotte pioneered his LAM, Layer Amplification Method, which allows each layer to be viewed at a time. Now it is possible to see each and every mark Da Vinci made (and erased) along the way to completing his masterpiece. Being able to see what is hidden also fascinated me and seemed particularly relevant given our tumultuous political climate where decisions are hidden. The pentimenti felt to me to be symbols of power, hidden as well as seen or felt. Seeing marks that the artist made five centuries ago was so powerful, as though I have been allowed into the studio of the artist where no one has seen those paint marks since the early 1500's. Power of the human touch as well as the lusting of humans for overpowering political power just kept me awake and thinking. I decided that I would appropriate the pentimenti but since it was already totally out of its original context, I would use each marking as I pleased. Taking these marks completely out of their context (which no one alive since early 1500s would know anyway) allowed me the artistic freedom to place them in my own painting as they were most effective visually. Using different colors for each set of markings and using individual placement I played around until I felt I had something visually compelling (at least to me!). This took awhile!! It was no longer a portrait of anyone specific, yet my own personal joyful journey and indictment of political power made in secret. My painting is a base of spray painting that in and of itself took weeks and weeks to finalize. I kept tweaking the layers of spray paint until I was happy with it as a base. I wanted it to be very fuzzy, very soft to create a sense of space so that the oil paint markings that go on top create a sharp set of lines that bring the viewer to view the piece as a sense of space.

I have followed Pascal Cotte and his company Lumiere Technology since he first photographed the *Mona Lisa* for the Louvre in 2003. I was intrigued at that time by the way Cotte was able to pinpoint each specific pigment by its spectral resonance and know what pigments Da Vinci used when painting *Mona Lisa*. I guess knowing the rules allows you the freedom to know when to break them in order to achieve a dissonance in the painting on purpose in order to create something new, which is what I am after. I've decided that context is everything and yet completely subjective once you remove it and in a painting that can be beautiful.

http://www. susanlizotte.com

Suzanne Budd

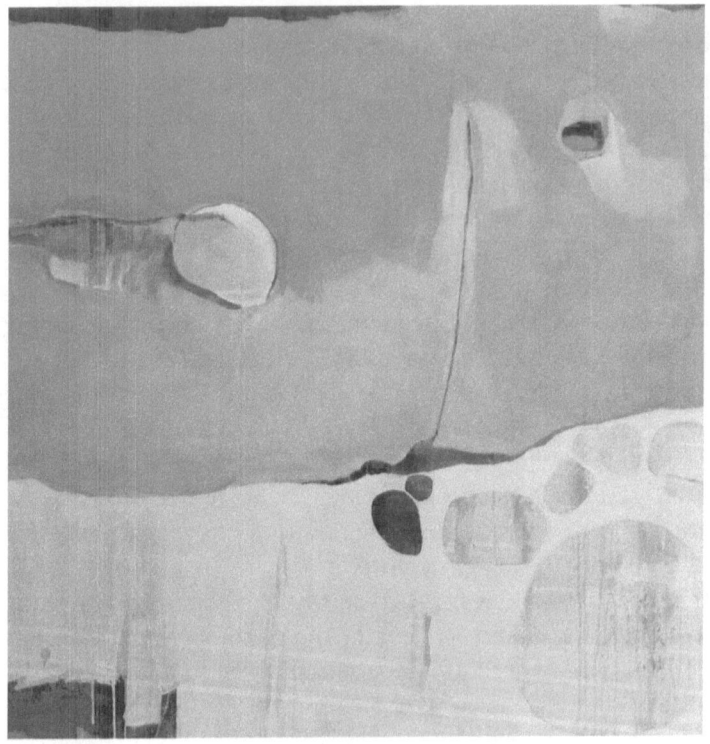

Memory Stones

Visitation Stones

2016 is the year stones began appearing in my paintings. Rocks, stones and stone walls have been calling to me to pay attention to them for a few years now. I visited Israel for the first time in 2015 and was powerfully affected by Jerusalem's many stone walls and how the stones nestle together creating community; each stone equally important in maintaining the structure and strength of the wall. I began to reflect on the significance of stones and of community. There is a common Jewish custom of leaving a visitation stone at the grave site of a loved one. This custom of leaving small visitation stones became a symbolic gesture over time; a way for the visitor to say to the loved one, "I love you and remember you."

My mother, sister and I left my birthplace, Fredericton, New Brunswick, Canada when I was 12 years old, 4 years after the death of my father. After our departure for Los Angeles, other family members took on the responsibility of visiting my father's grave site and putting stone on top of his gravestone. To this day, many decades later, there are few family members still alive or residing in Fredericton but I hope that someone from the Shul goes to the only Jewish cemetery and places stones on my father's gravestone.

In 2016 I was fortunate to visit Prague in the Czech Republic. Hauntingly beautiful, the Old Jewish Cemetery in the Jewish Quarter of Old Town Prague has tumbling down, old gravestones. It feels like existing in a world with nothing but gravestones and almost every monument has stones resting on top; small and big, nestled together or layered one upon another, just resting there seeming to hold all of our cumulative memories. It's a very moving experience. Again, I felt the presence of community with more than 100,000 bodies buried here since 1478. There are about a dozen tiers reportedly existing beneath the visible markers. The gravestones are placed tightly together, some tilting and leaning on their neighbor, others standing upright and some of the older, more fragile of the group toppled to the ground. Reportedly, ghosts from every century have been seen by visitors.

The painting I've submitted titled "Memory Stones" is an abstract landscape prominently featuring stones. I hadn't planned on stones but there they are. There is a demarcation between below ground and above ground. The demarcation has the deepest, most intense rich red color, resting on the earth while below ground two small red stones start their descent. The other stones below ground are delicate and fading, nestled closely together while above ground the stones appear to be strong and full of vitality. The thin vertical tendril above ground seems to be reaching upwards providing continuity between present time and a time before. To me this relates to how our existence rests on the history of our ancestors. There is some evidence of the history of the painting in the top left area and in the bottom left area where the most recent layers leave the previous layers exposed. I was not consciously aware of any of this while I was painting. I was ONLY painting. I love the immersive quality of painting and out of that process there are always discoveries.

www.suzannebudd.com

Tomoaki Shitbata

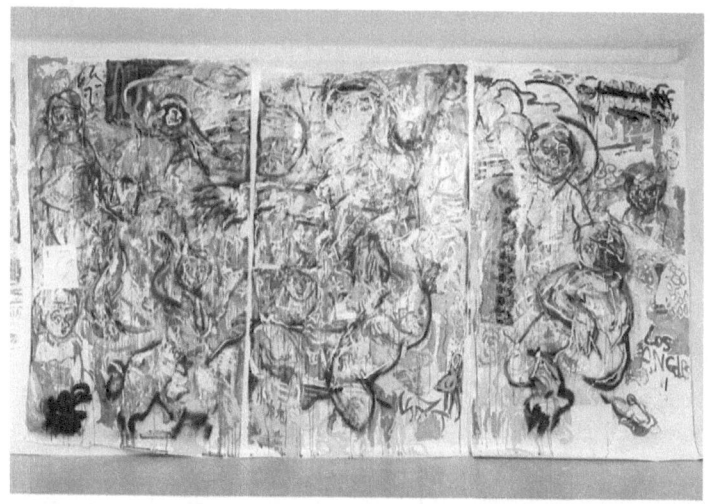

Big Blue

Big Blue Painting

I will journal one my painting and the background here. I exposed this large painting at a group show in LA Artcore Brewery Annex in December 2016 "Direct Translation". This article is a fragment of the LA art history reflecting my reality in 2016 because the group show was so difficult that it was dramatic. I cannot stop shooting my mouth off my personal opinion should be packed in closet. It was an experience. Everybody know challenging experience is food of the life, and the artist's one would forever tell a fact in the art history describing a process an artist get successful. I gained friend-ships or institutional power in deep ways.

This one image shown I created it as a mobile mural. Because I like Chicano art. The height is 105". The total width of the 3 paintings is 180". It is one of the biggest works I made in the US in 2016. Nancy provided me Nova paint. She is a known Japanese American artist living in artist district for ages. The paint she gave me was blue. So the painting got blue.

I love LA Artcore and the community. The show was a group show. I and several visual artists including Pranay Reddy exposed new works. I was charged in installing my works in the third gallery space. I forgot the number of works I brought but I tucked and hung them all over the walls. They were posters, paintings and drawing. The reason why I did expose very much many works there was easy. Just wanted to. I had stayed in LA for 2 years but exhibition opportunity was so rare. Most Americans may not understand how difficult and important to hang abroad. It was just that my desire bombed.

TOS is a three artists' collaboration group where I have been since 2016. TOS physically and psychologically helped me. The image photo was taken by Sarah Park. She is a member. TOS is a multi cultural artists unit of Tomoaki Shibata, Ozaman Yıldırın and Sarah Park. We met in a language school in Koreatown. We are co-making a film art. Ozaman and Sarah visited that LA Artcore group show and take pictures. Sarah helped uninstalling at the last day. TOS is independent and young. I am a Japanese painter, Ozaman is a Turkey video artist, and Sarah is a Korean photographer.

Efrain Maltinez is an artist from Oxaca. He visited me on the group show and we talked first time. I contacted him on line when I saw his painting in my neighbor restaurant, Vees Coffee, Miracle Mile. His painting was my type. A guy whom I asked about Efrain in the restaurant told me he has a TV show in Dromebox. The name is Eskwilax Hour. It broadcast local artists' live painting performance online. I appeared this TV twice after we talked in front of this blue painting. I think he is a great artist.

I am lucky because I have friends helping me a lot. The experience was nice.

Tracey Weiss

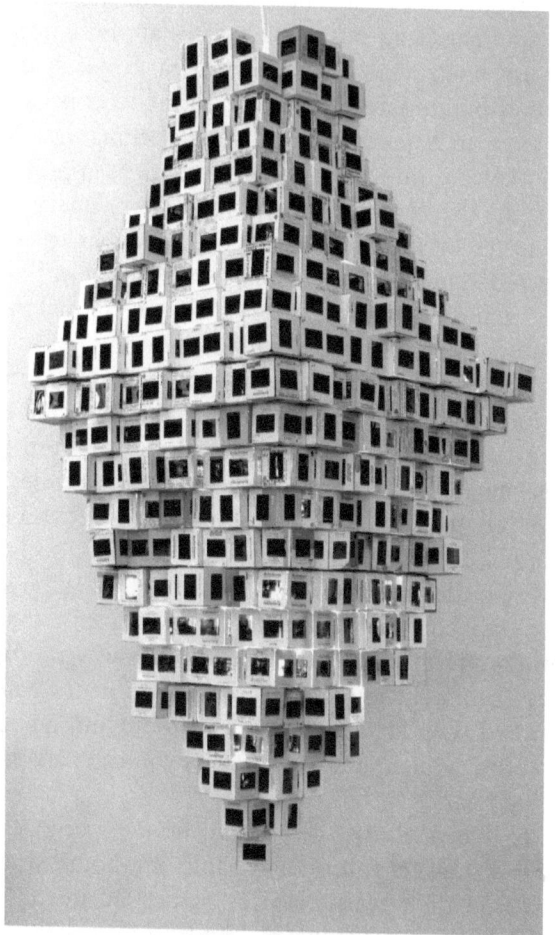

This Side Towards Screen

It was a hot July afternoon. I was teaching ceramics in summer school at a local community college, a lucky break for an artist that often is stuck with 3 months of unemployment every year. Through the bustling sound of students working and studio chatter, I heard a crashing sound outside my classroom. I poked my head outside to see what was happening and there was a dumpster sitting outside a neighboring room. A couple of people I didn't recognize, along with the dean were heaving metal drawers and old binders into the dumpster. It was the summer clean out. Since classes are minimum in the summer it's often a good time for extra projects, including binging and purging, to occur. My curiosity was peaked and I walked over to inspect the discarded belongings. When I peered inside the dumpster I was shocked. It appeared to be the entire art department's slide library! Every image that had been projected on the wall during an art history class was now sadly discarded in the giant receptacle. I inquired with the dean what was going on. He told me that they were making room and cleaning out "this room of junk". I continued to inquire and he elaborated on the obsolete nature of the slides now that everything is digital. I don't know why, but I was taken back and almost appalled. Obsolete? While I see the truth to what he was saying, it struck me as harsh words at the time. I asked if I could have the slides and he just looked at me with a some-what confused look and said, "sure....I guess so." Having absolutely no idea what I would do with all of these slides, I excitedly grabbed binders from the trash and started stacking them on the ground. Realizing this job was way too big, and they were absolutely not going to slow down their cleaning for me, I ducked back inside my own classroom and grabbed my two lab techs. "Quick, grab as much as you can carry and lets take it to my car!"

Later that day when I returned home, I unload all the binders and drawers full of slides into my home studio. All labeled. All in their plastic sleeves or nestled in the slots of their specialized metal drawers. I had no idea what I would do with them; I just knew they couldn't simply be discarded as common trash. Slides bring back memories. For some, memories of childhood, vacations, and family slide shows. For me they bring back memories of college and my early days in the art world. Days of shooting my own work on slide film as well as sending off slides, and sometimes even carousels, to graduate schools and galleries. I entered the art world at that sliver of time in between slides and digital. I applied to graduate school with slides, but documented my graduate show in digital media. I well remember putting together slide shows for my classes in school, and even for my first couple years of teaching.

I'd been working in found materials the last few years, so the idea wasn't new to me, thought the slides themselves as an art medium were. After playing around with them for a while, I started building with them. Although they were somewhat limiting, I found the slides intriguing. . The work took on an architectural feel that I really liked. After continuing to build with the materials in this architectural manner, the result ended with my first slide sculpture. I found the slides quite interesting the more I worked with them. While they are all seemingly the same, tiny images incased in white frames or cardboard or plastic, they were all quite unique. The diversity of images, of course, but also I became captivated by the labels on the mounts. Many of them typed, but many hand written with a variety of information: Titles, dates, artists, even "property of". The one common phrase that I saw over and over again staring at these peculiar little objects became the title of the final work: "This Side Towards Screen". Not only an exciting piece for me at the time, this sculpture let me to a whole new body of work that I continue working on today.

www.traceyweissart.com

Randi Matushevitz

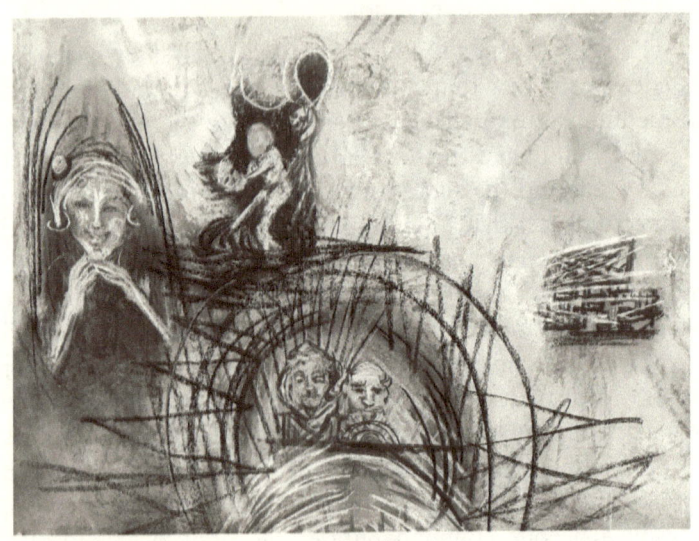

Sunday Drive

2016 A Year of Rediscovery

"Sunday Drive" invites the viewer to experience the shine of the ordinary. Of course there is no ordinary, only it's perception. This idea of perception is the perfect lead-in for sharing my story of 2016. It was a lull for my artistic life. I made plenty of work that lived in my flat files. Until my niece introduced me to a curator who's generosity and encouragement would help change my perception of myself as an artist. In January I had my first solo show in Los Angeles, "Mysterious" at UCLA Hillel, thank you to Perla Karney. Perla encouraged me to "get out of the closet, the art closet", and I did. She introduced me to artists, curators, and artist groups. I am grateful for her encouragement.

The year continued to be full of surprises and adventures and most importantly hard work. Multi-tasking is the life style of the artist. Not only did I make the work, I had to write and talk about it. Over the year I began navigate Los Angeles and its very spread out art community, updated my website and social media, and began going to galleries and art events, and meeting other artists. I joined Los Angeles Art Association (LAAA) and Jewish Artists Initiative (JAI), joined a critique group, entered lost of competitions, got in a few shows, got invited to a few shows (thank you Karrie and Eric). I'd like to give a shout out to Kristine Shomaker for her continued guidance and support through out this process.

2016 was the year that I will look back on as live changing. I rediscovered myself, as ARTIST. I continue to work daily in my studio. I have made a career of looking for opportunities and artistic development. My perception of my life has shifted. I'm thrilled to be in Los Angeles, a city filled with opportunities for art and artists. I am grateful for all the artists and art professionals that I am meeting and working among...

Thank you Karrie Ross for documenting our work and our moment in time.

www.RandiMatushevitz.com

Karrie Ross

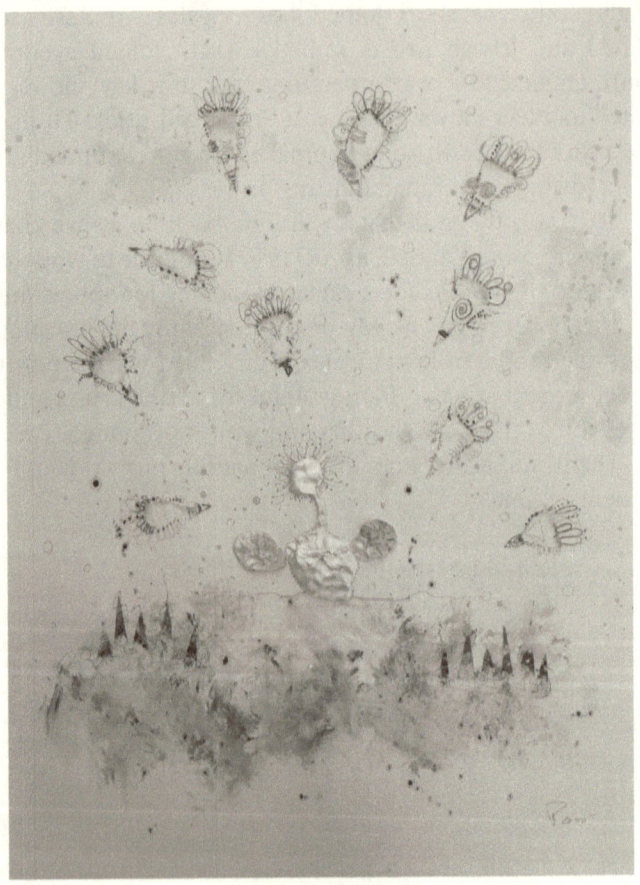

Where is the Water?

2016.
A year of lots of change.
Change in my location
Change in my living dynamic
Change in my health
Change in my everything it seems as I try to write about it.

I started the year getting used to the new home I now have. Its really nice, cozy and safe. Safe. That's a different word than many are used to hearing or even saying. Safe.

Safe from ...? Of course it's a personal perspective, and shows up differently for each of us and in the end is just another illusion we create for ourselves. Some need to feel safe in their relationship, or job, or appearance —but the most uncomfortable are the ones protecting a perceived self importance, control of others — these are what I call "Bullies". I have been exposed to many bully-types over my lifetime. They are not a fun experience, and each has their own way, and degree of bullying. Unfortunately I realize, to me, that their attitude is their way of feeling safe, a perceived feeling of being more powerful than another. HOWEVER it does not make it right to bully others in private or public. For petesake wake up! I have learned the hard way that if I bring these actions to their attention it only makes them more incessed with "getting back" at me for the wrong they imagine I've done to them. I do not need someone blaming me for the whatevers...

I never realized just how much I needed to feel 'safe' until I got hit with a large company coming after my trademark — and my world started to crumble, and I needed help. I didn't understand the language, process, accusations that were coming at me, and I had no funds to fight it.

I tried a lawyer who really was no help, and expensive.

I tried the non profit lawyer association—they didn't have a clue, didn't listen, took too long, and thought that just any lawyer would do...!

I offered several times to pay lawyers for an hours worth of info... they just laughed at me and told me to give my property to the bully! Yeah really...?

Then I tried LinkedIn... ha ha ha...

I was at a loss.

I realized I would have to contact the lawyer of the company coming after me. That I would have to deal with this myself. I really needed help. WOW. Scary and was certainly not a safe feeling. I kept suggesting to them the name they chose was awful and I would help them with a new brand. I've created brands for over 40 years in one way or another. For some reason the company just had to have access and control over my name.

I finally learned a lot more about the legal aspects of what was happening, and over time found a little help in the USPTO help line. They directed me to the procedures and sequence of events and warned me of the horror of not following through. Every waking hour for 9 months and I finally realized that the other persons agreement they proposed wanted me to lie. I do no lie. And I would be lying under oath and to the Directors of the USPTO but mostly to me and my over-reactive conscience. I told them I was going to take it all the way unless they dropped it. The bully tried and tried one last time to scare me but once I had enough knowledge to at least keep ahead of them, felt secure in my existing rights, and I knew I could start over if I had to, they could not win. I would not back down.

I realized that getting into the head of the bully was what I had to do, whether I agreed with them or not, I needed to figure out how they perceived life, their thoughts, and re-evaluated what my home, my 'safe' meant to me. Not to be mean, but to be resolved in my actions.

I eventually wore them down. They finally withdrew the lawsuit. I still have PTSD about this and I have not been able to bring myself to check the status of my trademark.

Life presents situations all the time. Keep your ears open and your mouth asking questions. Objectivity. Observation.

The art "Where is the Water?" presented a look at how stressed out I was, lots of arrows pointing at me as I flutter in the mist of a sea of mountians. 30"x22", mixed media.

Then through all this, the Presidential elections were going on and the debates were being taken over by the biggest demeaning, childish, ignorant, Bully and manipulator I have ever seen — Wait... not really, but they are much larger and grander in scale then those that I've experienced in my life, but a Bully just the same. What their being elected tells me is that there are lots of people out there feeling like victims just waiting for the Bully.

http://www.karrierossfineart.com
http://www.oureverchangingworld.com